T0381166

Blissful Vibes

Our Euphoric Moments of Laughter

PJ Karr, Ph.D.

Archway Publishing books may be ordered through booksellers or by contacting:

Archway Publishing
1663 Liberty Drive
Bloomington, IN 47403
www.archwaypublishing.com
844-669-3957

Photography by: PJ Karr, Ph.D.

ISBN: 978-1-6657-3916-0 (sc)
ISBN: 978-1-6657-3917-7 (e)

Library of Congress Control Number: 2023902976

Print information available on the last page.

Archway Publishing rev. date: 03/15/2023

Contents

**Embark on a daily mission to find our misplaced laughter
and a prime chance for the merriment…**

Dedications

Arlene...

My college buddy and sister-friend of fifty years who remains smitten with our lucid daydreaming, the rowdy playtime, and our quest to snatch the hilarity on any day, week, month, or year. Namaste...

Madre and JJ...

My earliest mentors and the gift-givers of the laughter that resonated from a deep abyss of my belly. I shall never forget. Love, sweet love...

Acknowledgments

I was appreciative and grateful for two decades of quirky hilarity with Pete. His contagious cackling, whether he was being corny or hysterical, added a unique zest to our world. His blissful vibes enriched and uplifted any individuals in his presence. Keep enjoying the heavenly bliss, Pete!

Jeffie, a smashing exemplar of the streaming cackles, offered a treasure trove of laugh goodies. As a best buddy in high school and college years, I never forgot our weeks. We were teasing, joking, or half-trying to control our ruckus laughter. Many years later, I moved back to New England and we visited. He still owned that wondrous stream of cackles. Cheerio for the natural highs, Jeffie!

Beej, my middle sister, was always in sync with my illustrious raves. Her laughter, usually at a moment's notice, would morph into unmistakable laugh snorts. Immediate adoption of her entertaining, comical virtue? No worries, as I re-enacted this sensational laugh-snorting in her presence, and thereafter, in my whimsical scenarios. High-five's and our wagging baby fingers, my treasured Beej!

Antonio, a rousing and a passionate companion, exuded his dynamic, fervent belly laughs at certain moments. His look-at-me scenarios created the countless ripple effects for myself. In my forever bucket list, *laughing togetherness* lingered as our ultimate gift. Indeed, no price tag, Antonio!

Arlene, a determined and a vivacious spirit, contributed to our evolving friendship. For five-plus decades, she continued to be my lucid daydreamer and an incredible beamer of the lighter fares in our life safari. My golden goblet runneth over, my sister-friend, Arlene!

Acknowledging thousands of my collegiate students, representing diverse stages of life and the multicultural endowments, resonated in my heart. I beamed "then" and even beamed "now" with a lustrous light. Thank you for welcoming our gamut of universal laughter, good will, and indulgence during our stimulating, refreshing, and intriguing classes.

We were the team players, concocting the untold funnies during a melee of classes, campus events, and a potpourri of parking-lot pleasures. My forever gift-givers and gatekeepers of the light, I still adored celebrating and honoring all of you!

Life is a Celebration

Partake of the life moments that are upbeat, unforgettable, and priceless...

Introduction

Life moments are upbeat, unforgettable, and priceless. Dazzling celebrations, an exceptional day or week, and an illustrious year contribute to our evolving legacy. Other daily memories begin to magnify, morphing in another direction. Our global pandemic, unresolved crises in our personal journeys, or the breaking-news forecasts become our imprints as well.

No mystification or any bewilderment as to why we humans seek a relief, a palliative comfort, or our wanton reprieves. Pursuing something else that comforts us is not rocket science. We envision a realm of possibilities. Hobbies, aerobic workouts, and new avenues that offer a welcome intermission from our daily stressors are quite prominent.

One choice is left behind, either unintentionally or somehow forgotten. Do any of us realize how much? Our opportunities for amusement, a vibrant hilarity, and our playtime represent the inestimable comforts and our astounding rejuvenations.

Feisty, outrageous, witty, zesty, and mischievous traits coax mystically. They seduce the marvelous, non-toxic "stuff" in our life—the smiles, a har-de-har, and an authentic fire in our belly. According to the credible researchers, these traits are guaranteed to resuscitate our cracking up and feeling super-duper, rather than our dreaded doldrums or a perpetual disquiet.

Feel free to reflect, head nod, and grin. Entice any of the misplaced, lost-and-found, and humorous experiences—past, present, or envisioned in the near future. The *present* is a better and higher quality option.

When we desire these ruckus noises from a subterranean abyss of our belly, these "natural highs" transform into the best medicine. No urgency for any doctors to keep validating these findings. Absolute sovereignty sways us. Enough of us become infatuated and primed for what needs to happen.

We eyeball and take part in the humorous scenarios that make plenty of room for our amusement, the inspirational joy, and our vigorous chuckles. Any place or any time sounds restorative. Our mirth and gleeful pleasures are already documented as totally awesome for our mind and heart.

We yearn for something else besides our praise or the raves for our newest, heightened awareness. Eventually, our regular participation and heading for a personal gusto translates to an enviable guarantee. A phenomenal circulation, top-notch healing, and a mighty immune system become our realities.

There are *positive* changes in our immune system with the avid pursuits of our daily doses of humor. Vamoose—to any negative vibes, our leftover worries, or a perpetual angst. We choose to snatch a few minutes and opt to change today's momentum.

Let's surmise that we pause to reflect momentarily about laughing as an aerobic workout. How long? Fifteen or twenty-five seconds is like a three-minute, vigorous workout. Plus, our core muscles adore the giggles.

After our laugh-aerobic workout, it is high time to chill. Just breathe naturally from our diaphragm, pause throughout that day, and idolize that harmonic balance. Succumb to every tidbit of our heightened laughs.

There is another light-bulb insight. Our "hmm" is humbling, especially whenever we hear the simple answer.

Laughter is a freebie. All of today's medicinal hoopla about our snickers, giggles, and fantastic bellyaches is not complex, convoluted, or puzzling. Just make a choice—lighten up! Our lost-and-found giggles, chuckles, and tummy vibrations are easy to manifest, according to the crème de crème researchers. Today's professionals tell it like it is.

Hey, any sourpusses out yonder, now is a perfect time to lighten up. Take a break and look into a mirror. Yes, find a mirror, preferably the big-kahuna size. Make the worst sourpuss faces—a ton of them. Laughing or snickering while watching these crazed mirror-images?

According to contemporary gurus and guruettes, these intentional pauses for our outlandish antics and laughter are a sure bet. Must we squeeze in this quality time for our playtime, the hilarity, or the shared laughter in our life?

Absolutely! Voodoo on no changes or the leftovers from any negative lens, while viewing our status of living large. Never say never.

This bizarre, engaging behavior is our golden parachute with another upbeat, promising perk. We feel a welcome transformation from a case of the terminal sourpuss. Purposeful stretches to change our negative lens defuse a concoction of our tiresome daily or weekly stressors.

We grant permission for this laughter mission. We wipe out those annoying, must-do lists. Yadda, yadda, yadda. Our infamous lists preserve and bolster a daily feeding frenzy.

Delete button, where art thou? It is far better to nourish these golden perks with our laughter mission.

Simple reminders from today's sage advisors who own the crystal ball on better health predications are handy. First, love or at least adore that the ecstasy and our giggles are numero uno. They are a top priority of what needs to happen every day, not once a year or in our wildest dreams. Second, be ready to blast off for a never-never land of playful merriment. Third, become a diehard who witnesses, deserves, and scouts out playtime as a daily habit. How about a first-rate hint?

When needed, pause and look closely. Acknowledge one truth in a heart throb. Most children are committed. They are the wiser owners of bellyache leftovers from their sublime to exotic trails of daily giggles. How do they fare each day?

Most children laugh 145 times each day. Guess what the average number is for adults? Well, most adults want to forget or dismiss my pop quiz routine. Ready or not, here comes an eminent and relevant wake-up call.

Most adults laugh only four times per day. Is this only on our bad hair or grumbling-mumbling days? Yet, higher than four daily doses are in the stars for us (a.k.a. the *extraordinary* adults). What about the potentially fewer times for the not-so-enlightened adults (not me or you, of course)?

Zap. The wicked witch does exist. It is her fault, all her fault. Where is the fairy godmother to grant our desperado wish for the ultimate humor? We want to chuckle, snicker, snort, chortle, guffaw, grin, or roar with our outrageous howls.

Wait a blasted minute. We need to chuckle or at least smirk at the absurdity of most adults losing ground since their childhood days.

With all due respect, the newest research remains a no brainer. Deep in our heart and soul, many of us feel confidant or certain. It is superior karma to seek and find our laughter on any day, week, month, or year.

Do a majority of adults seize the day? Do we head for that birth of mirth? Is this beneficial, medicinal hoopla a bona fide foreshadowing?

What about our huge leap: 145 times for our giggle meter? Everything becomes a dangling carrot. Well, why not?

No fretting or negative judgements are warranted. We adults rise to the occasion. Embark on a daily mission to find our misplaced or invisible laughs and our humorous antics. Our pauses to watch and play an instigator of the wild-thang moments are spectacular, soulful, and healthy.

Resurrect an inventive and bodacious character to sustain our creative or outrageous playtime. Listen to the gossip (pardon, now the famous research) about laughter as a stress defuser. Embrace that our daily amusements make a quality difference in our attitude *and* our altitude.

Meanwhile back at the ranch, my PJ moments kept reappearing. Was I delusional? Was I becoming a blissful sponsor for our lost-and-found chuckles and the notorious instigator of let 'em rip?

Well, I felt a soulful urgency to kick-start our "go for it" motto. It was in the cards, the stars, or our universe. Go forth as a full-fledged, universal sponsor and a proud instigator on behalf of our adult laughter.

I felt another rush of equal urgency and repute. My intrinsic desire was to "pay forward" the healthy benefits of humor, merriment, and those blissful vibes.

Beware, young children and attentive youth. The adults reading this book or the diehards spreading our newsflashes about cheerfulness raise the bar for our hilarity. No more titanic losses of daily laughter for us adults, especially when we commit, seek, and reaffirm the "go for it" motto.

The infamous crystal ball is working on our behalf. There are unpredictable, zany moments. Interested adults risk-take, not just the children or youth. These adult-kiddos become the real instigators for these time outs and making up for the missed opportunities.

I pursued my irrepressible inclination to divulge tempting stories to recapture our lost-and-found, laughing quota of 145 times per day. Daily experiences with a prime chance for snickers and laughs from a deeper abyss were present, persuasive, and addictive.

Are several of us dashing to move from feeling a little depressed or off a bubble to soaring higher, like the amazing eagles? Lighten-up shifts our gears to a happier, elevated mood.

This latest newsflash, the crème de crème of present research, confirms that our brains are not rigid. Exonerate and free the oldie-moldy ways of thinking. Now is high time to retrain the brain, especially to liberate our humor, the enlightenments, and our positive outcomes.

Fortunately, we adults are wired, on the brink, and anticipating these refreshing moments. We yearn, crave, and make the well-deserved room for our adult playtime.

By the way, ever met anyone who wants to feel a melancholy, be unhappy, or be miserable? For many of us, playfulness is a far better choice.

A return to our blissful vibes and the euphoric laughs from an omnipotent and robust abyss of our belly switches to a serenity. Our mind, body, and spirit are lifted upward.

In a commanding and glorious way, our life becomes cinematic. These days of our life become an impressive awakening with a purposeful, strong-willed choice for our unique and outstanding playtimes.

Kudo Dog

Sisterhood and brotherhood are regal destinations,
A blossoming fellowship of ecstasy, playtime, and abundance,
Positive attitudes and today's sustenance create a softer repose…

Dearest Mother Nature rules the roost. Entering our cozy coffee shop that was bustling, I spotted a cafe table near the front window and scurried there. I finished our scrumptious order, right before my best friend arrived.

"Yay! Got our favorite table and ordered our treats," I boasted, as we hugged and giggled like adorable kiddos.

"Cheerio!" we flaunted in sync, as both of us sat down with our lavish grins.

As dear friends, we were a winning team, clicking our piping hot mugs filled with an aromatic Sumatra blend. We munched and savored the cranberry-nut muffins, almost as much as our nostalgic rendezvous.

Our cushy seats were close to a window sill near the front window. Was it marvelous karma to secure this bird's eye view? Indeed, given my recent goal to raise my giggle-meter to at least 100 times per day. My best friend and I were destined to succumb. We became the prime witnesses effortlessly.

Conversing at the nearby sidewalk were two, bundled-up individuals with a pooch. We gave one another our famed, wide-eyed stares and began to laugh heartily.

"Either their winter attire is triple-layered or they are definitely from Alaska," I quipped, as our heads bobbled in unison. "Hey, their pooch on a leash owns an obvious chutzpah!"

My endearing friend raised our laugh meter with her quick wit and retort. "In my next reincarnation as a dog, I would bypass any barking and choose a flamboyant howl with these brr temperatures!"

Not so with this stoic pooch. His doggie standstill hit the max potential. Suddenly, it was high time for a doggie chill-test. Attempts to rest his buttocks on the frigid cement resulted in the exotic, spring-loaded jumps and fancy twirls. The gawking and hysterical groupies, seated in our busier cafe, stopped to eyeball this stupendous doggie.

Our countless outbursts of laughter, clapping, and finger-pointing guaranteed a larger audience. Several of us gawked at this riveting and engaging show, ramping up our next opportunities for at least forty to fifty doses of tee-heeing.

My loco peals of laughter reverberated in this cozy cafe. I validated that this pooch deserved an Oscar namesake.

"Hooray, Kudo Dog!" I proclaimed, applauding and joshing with my best friend and several folks within earshot.

Well, the kudos for my friend, myself, and our kindred spirits were warranted as well. Was I on target or what—calling the utmost attention to this befitting and worthy "Kudo Dog." Spot on!

During the last decade, there were increased health endorsements to defuse regularly. Adults needed to oust that nasty cortisol and epinephrine that kerplunked into our bodies, given the higher doses of our daily, frenzied living.

A purposeful, pivotal detour was paramount. Hanging tight with a person or a group that enticed our gaiety, a joie de vivre, and hilarity, like the splendor of this cafe experience, was invaluable.

Inevitably, a day for another grateful affirmation arrived. Alas, children were not the only ones with a natural desire to let loose and giggle. We adults were equally as capable of such an "endorphin high" on any day, week, or month.

Which playful friends would be chosen? I revered my longtime friend and our get-togethers at this cozy cafe. Today, when the "Kudo Dog" entertainment evolved, these charming, tantalizing, and engrossing pursuits were not shunned. All of us seized the day—Carpe Diem—with our healthier, humorous scenario.

Our coffee groupies were mesmerized. Each of us was in stitches and on the same page. The entertaining scenario evolved into a crowning time to high-five and to give "Kudo Dog" his standing ovation.

I was feeling smug, willing to embrace today's dramatic comedy hour. Best of all, I instigated and accepted the contagious spirit that spread like an untamed, wild fire in our cafe.

We adults surpassed the lowly and meager statistics of four times per day, particularly when we indulged in today's hilarity. We raised the bar, upped the ante for today's statistics. Whoopee, rah-rah, and three cheers…

At a moment's notice, I conjured up these images of our grand finale that day at our bustling cafe. There was a dynamite broadcast of "Accolades for Kudo Dog" followed by our teary eyes, the enthusiastic applause, and our titanic belly laughs.

Now, there was another pause. I wondered who else witnessed and enjoyed "Kudo Dog" on a different day or week.

In the interim, my best friend and I made a pact. We promised to return with our fervent and zealous hopes of witnessing "Kudo Dog" and his next doggie chill-test.

HAPPY THOUGHTS

Embrace the crowning moments to high-five and laugh during today's comedy...

Refreshing Moments

Be a jesting, light-hearted junkie to attain a chill-out nirvana,
Snafu the split-second liberations and an indelible rejuvenation,
Be smug, let go, and hail these bodacious moments…

We do not have to become the stand-up comics. Yet, there is an obvious need to pursue the lighten up quests and stumble upon the daily funnies that permit us to feel elevated and splendiferous.

Why? To move forward from any realm of a daily angst, the years of diverse national and global concerns, and the complexity of our pandemic mutations. Our refreshing moments are much appreciated and stellar in any season.

For myself, it was an early summer day. I pursued my inspiration and longing to head for a nearby lake and indulge. Been there…done that?

The cooler, spring-fed lake did not stop the wannabe swimmers. They headed for that old-fashioned plunge, followed by the lightening-quick strokes with the swimming splurges. I paused to listen and snicker.

"Oh, MAN!" Then a hoot or the lavish and bizarre howls.

"Swim FAST!" Other beach enthusiasts followed suit, including myself.

"YIKES! C'mon, Patricia!" I managed to yell, only pausing for a millisecond. She hovered at the shore, only up to her knee caps and waving wildly. I knew that was wild enough for Patricia, especially on this early summer day at our nostalgic, spring-fed lake.

I swam back swiftly and full tilt to the shoreline in the generous sunbeams. Patricia already ran to get the two beach towels.

"Look. Our TOWELS! Swim faster-r-r," she shouted, enticing our infinite giggles. "You are so brave or very…" Patricia initiated, only to break off into her riotous, entertaining cackles again.

"Whew, what a blast from my past! Invigorating and my *beastly* idea!" I confessed, my teeth chattering between my pursed lips and the obvious waves of shivers and quivers.

"Your lips are so PURPLE!" Both of us were laughing deliriously and bolted back to our warm and balmy blanket.

Wrapped in our gargantuan towels, we chatted and eyeballed the amusements. Other swimmers and their beelines to the shore became the first of today's comic reliefs. An appearance of the slapstick comedians, sporting an attitude to brave the spring-fed lake, came in nanoseconds. Different adults, teens, and children revealed a gala, feisty spirit with the impressive beach games.

The wind whispered gently through the majestic pines. Building sand castles and burying a certain someone— one's body, feet, and only up to a Chinny-chin-chin— became a pure jubilance for all of us. Then one group, boldly air-drying and playing frisbee in the golden rays of sunshine, stopped to feast their eyes upon the waterfront.

Most of us remembered "the one." He or she insured our sidesplitting, hold-your-stomach storytelling for weeks. Most toddlers were being watched carefully, but fate took its course with one tyke. In a flash (no pun intended), this toddler was giggling and beaming at her nudity.

Mom smiled sheepishly while trying to pull, tug, and desperately yank up her child's wet bottoms. Picture the next funnies. The child's bottoms continued to cling tenaciously around her pudgy, stick-um legs.

Here came the raucous laughs and clapping from our chipper beach audience. Then this toddler turned to us with her wide grin and contagious giggles—ready to start all over again.

Today promoted an astonishing karma. The adult-kiddos went far beyond the average laughter dose of four times daily. The enthused kids lived up to their masterful, envied reputation of 145 giggles galore.

All of us soared exponentially with our mega-doses of laughter. Our hilarity was magical, influencing our ultimate and the *refreshing moments* on that inviting, early summer day.

Laughter is the Best Elixir

Learning a lore of play, we humans gain,
Stashing the memories, fantastic for our wanton brain,
Imprinting the joys, our hearts buoyant again…

I came out of the doctor's office. Little did I know, as I fiddled in my Euro pouch, trying to fetch my Galactica Goddess car keys. Hmm, found everything else, but not my car keys.

So, why did I even glance across the parking lot? Clueless!

My unexpected moments were forthcoming. A golden retriever and a snow-white poodle rested their heads atop the back seat of a swanky convertible, enjoying their open-air day.

These dogs began to stare sweetly, as if they already knew. I needed a mega boost, given my doctor appointment. Just envision—their captivating, doggie eyes from that posh convertible parked in the shade. Suddenly, the whispering winds of time made their groomed fur move ever so gently.

I started to talk to them. They casted their beholden eyes, much like the gifted "empaths" (doggie gifts, I believe). Heads raised slightly, they listened attentively to every word and my intermittent giggles. They offered the utmost, unconditional attention to my PJ-doggie minutes.

"Oh, hi there, you dazzling doggies! So comfy, I imagine. Wassup? I bet you have fabulous stories of folks who stopped to chat. You are living large!" I crooned, grinning and taking in these relaxing minutes.

Then I heard another person's voice, somewhere yonder in this parking lot. "Hey, elegant dogs! Are you enjoying the day? Just look at both of you. How charming!"

I smiled and chuckled again, the warm fuzzies overtaking my mind and spirit. I drove home on the back roads, keeping that PJ-doggie imagery stored in my memory bank.

My melodic laughs and doggie commentary were stashed in the epicenter of my belly. I was ready to retrieve today's warm fuzzies at a moment's notice.

That afternoon transformed my earlier doctor appointment. My angst and mind-boggling worries morphed into a grin, my laughter, a pure enjoyment, and my distinctive bliss.

Perhaps, it was like a loving-kind pat on my back or a rave review. Perhaps, the loving-empath moments with these doggies in the swanky convertible were meant to be.

I needed to recall that these loving-kind and spontaneous moments counted. I remembered—just pause, partake of my longer breaths, and relax.

Seek, discover, and stretch to sneak in a tidbit of humor. I transformed my tougher day. Voila`, I did not forget...

Begone, Road Rage

Newly hatched and unfledged comrades on our busy roads,
Bespeak the fathomless secrets of an unexpected whimsy,
Gift-giving of a brief playtime from the wise gods and goddesses of simple joys...

Thousands of us hear or experience the road rage on our highways. How about the latest newsflash? This road rage is ramping up in our towns and diverse suburbs. The unexpected u-turns and the zooming through the yellow or red traffic lights are in vogue.

Did we envision this faster pace or I-am-miffed syndrome in our daily life? There is no mystique that several of us yearn to lessen our stressors. Even today's health professionals advocate the value of slowing down. Our muscles relax when we defuse for a few hours, try yoga and the Zen moments, or brighten and pep up after a few jollies.

Begone, those bad-to-the-bone stress hormones. That nasty cortisol and epinephrine attempt to steal our show. No bewilderment as to why a much-needed reprieve from any road rage is appreciated.

Does our amnesty from this ramped-up phenomenon seem surreal? The non-believers hang with me, as I recreate my real scenario.

Visualize a red light at an intersection in my town. As the streetlight changes to green, the in-a-rush drivers of trucks, cars, or motorcycles put the pedal to the metal. Nobody is slowing down, much less pausing to blink their lights at me, although the ebb and flow of traffic creates intermittent opportunities to turn. My blinking directional, my polite desire to make a turn, seems to be unwelcome or ignored.

Is it the perfect moment for my pleas to the gods, goddesses, ascended masters, and my guardian angels? Is it time to emit my colossal sighs or the notorious grumbles, expecting two or more traffic light changes?

Gotcha, PJ! Here comes my unexpected happening. Perhaps, it is an illusion.

Wait... A waving arm is stuck out a truck window, beckoning me to turn. Then flashing headlights signal another invitation. Alas, PJ—it is my turn! All of this happens without an impending fender-bender.

Remember? Vaguely?

There were usually smug grins and jovial chuckles. What did you really say or think? So, you did not resort to the expletives. Your blood pressure did not fly off the charts.

I had at least one confession about my begone, road-rage experiences. From the driver's seat, my irresistible urge was to return a sign of thanks, like my excessive hand waves. The entirety brought forth the warm fuzzies, a real grin, and my gift of today's chuckles.

Want to lower our blood pressure? It happens as a spectacular swan dive after our bodacious laughter. Want our mundane mood to soar in a split-second with giggles? Both are can-do realities with a few laugh doses in the company of these begone, road-rage experiences.

Our immune system awaits an intentional boost from our hee-haw sounds. Morning, afternoon, or evening does not matter.

Hmm, was that driver supposed to see my thrilled-to-pieces hand waves or my biggie-sized grin at dusk or in the evening? Probably not… Yet, I was grateful for the liberal goodwill. My muse of the heart loved these happy-camper signals and my genuine expressions that came forth.

"You are my earth angel! Thanks."

Gratitude flowed from car to car, something akin to ESP. No kidding.

I relished these unanticipated moments. Road rage and a lack of congeniality were nowhere to be found. How cool that another earthling and I raised the bar.

Hey, those adult-laugh tallies were coming full circle. Bravissimo, my personal tallies were increasing. A Cheshire-cat grin was plastered on my face as I drove onward, content to own this gift of unexpected chuckles.

Imagine, no road rage. Acts of random kindness from the considerate, courteous, inviting, peachy-cordial, or gracious drivers were destined to spin our expectancies.

I savored that my laugh meter made a 360 degree turn. Hooray!

Engage in different experiences that offer light-filled reprieves and unexpected smiles…

Out of the Clear Blue

Anticipate a zany or the irresistible concoction of amusement,
Adore each of the crazed adventures that evolve,
Invite kindred humans to recollect their memoir of festive delights…

Are you chomping at the bit to discover or revive the adult-kiddo playtime and those funnies? Researchers encourage us with a resounding, "Yes, please do!"

The bonuses of humor are an ASAP immune boost for our body. They become magnificent upgrades for our mind and spirit. These credible endorsements warrant the undivided attention, whether near or far away from our homesteads.

When I decided to travel in the spirit of the pioneers (sic), the choice of a reasonably priced, older cabin or a motel with a kitchenette insured my fun-filled escapades. I anticipated and looked forward to at least two things: my vintage appreciation and the gotcha-PJ surprises.

I headed for New Hampshire, a mother-nature reprieve with the lake cabins. That summer was our COVID-19 and the new normal. Wearing masks and social distancing, no vaccines, and the de-foggers were required.

These inspections were a part of our "new normal" cleaning routine at diverse resorts in many states. Occupancy at our state resorts was limited to 60% capacity. The traditional amenities like pools, gyms, and groups activities were limited time slots or not open.

My isolated resort, knowing the owners, and a pop-up Airbnb with the only cabin on the lake were my supah (Boston accent, please) temptations. Plus, this summer turned out to be a hot, unusually humid July.

In June, I was telling my sister that I yearned to go back to our childhood days at our treasured lake reprieve. Booked with the regular guests and fewer cabins, the owners were equally surprised that I snagged the *only cabin* left for the rest of the summer. My aroused hubbub with my Airbnb snafu resonated with my sister as well.

"Guess what? My Airbnb post revealed a ditto: the *only week* and vintage cabin left for the *entire* summer. What were those chances? Hey, no coincidence!" I asserted to my sister, grinning and dancing in my free spirit moments. I paused for a millisecond. My sister added a similar caveat.

"It was meant to be, sister. So cool!" she responded, chuckling as I embellished my free spirit dance at our beach on a nearby, pristine lake with conservation land and trails. I paused momentarily to share my dramatic stare. She knew more newsflashes were forthcoming and grinned.

"The owners, the youngest daughter and her hubby, just sold the New Hampshire lodge and the last cabins. This was their last year to stay in the lodge and rent the few cabins!" I added, as I pranced closer to her beach chair with a melodramatic flair.

My sister smiled anew. I forged ahead with my prancing and the jive dancing. When I paused to reflect, a breathtaking karma came full circle.

"Imagine, she was my vacation buddy all those summers. Later, her hubby and she owned and ran our family haunt for three decades."

"Wow, I snagged that only week!" I touted again. I remained enthused and clapping with my no-coincidence keepsake.

My sister was invited to indulge, if her week became open for the nostalgic and unforeseen adventures. Fast forward…

My unforgettable get-away included a working-for-now refrigerator like our Nana's fridge. The cookware, dishes, and utensils were Feng Shui in their 1940s to 1960s glory. No dishwasher, just wash-and-dry-yourself for the meals during my miraculous and spellbinding week.

Mixed furnishings with a vintage character of whatever decade occupied my small, economical quarters. The week was a delightful memoir. The cabin was the same knotty pine wood from our family vacations. The screened porch still offered the best views and the sunset glories.

Due to our earlier stages of COVID, the owners suggested bringing my bedroom sheets and personal pillows. The small cottage was very clean, sanitized, and followed state protocols and Airbnb guidelines.

I recall my happy-camper giggles, as I took my mini-tour of my exclusive week of the only lake-front cabin. An intermittent WiFi was the update. My key was vintage style attached to an oval-shaped, green cottage #1. Another flashback came forth to enhance my clairvoyant, family-vacation memoir.

A small journal on the coffee table, not just the high-tech reviews, was a pleasure to read that evening. I added my flair, an enthused commentary and my pencil sketches at the end of my abundant week.

Perhaps a distant or recent memories are returning to tickle your funny bones? I am pretty sure that most of us agree that vintage abodes come with a 99.9% guarantee for lasting and uplifting impressions.

Our laugh-in-hindsight memorabilia is often recounted in the fine fellowship of like-minded travelers. Ready to compare the impressive anecdotes, chronicles, and our whoopee?

Another comical lark at my lake-front cabin was the bed. When I attempted to go to sleep, the mattress was short enough for my feet to pop out. Next merriment? Imagine a gurgle emanating from a dark lagoon, the unknown depths of the sink pipes in my kitchenette. Of course, the gurgle resonated only during the "wee hours" of each morning.

The stand-alone shower appeared to be up to par until my vigorous scrub time. Stand straight and pivot in this tiny cavern. Comical episodes were a diverting and a gut-busting happening throughout my stay.

Expect the unexpected. Lately, I found myself doting on the cliché "out of the clear blue" and my comic reliefs with this week-long excursion. Even the humane and compassionate researchers remind us that it is never too late to bid a fond adieu to our monotonous, blah, or any humdrum moods.

Try an upgrade. Greet each day with a grin-win mentality instead of pouting, venting only negative vibes, or moping. Reliving the "unexpected" charms or charisma in our stories is a kick-start in the right direction.

A bit of empathic advice, in case you have not opted for a chance to relive such stories. First, try out your significant others. Acquaintances smile strangely. Strangers secretly think you are in La-La land.

In spite of the odds, make a bit of a fuss about your inventive storytelling. "While staying at this vintage cottage, you could not even pipe dream or scheme mischievously what really happened..."

It is destiny. No voodoo or any of the bad juju. Your animated storyteller takes over. Do you notice that an embellishment of the inconceivable moments just happens naturally?

With our storytelling, the ruckus laughter and good times roll again. Of course, there is the better or our best-ever news.

Those measly statistics for our adult laughter? The high numbers charge way out of bounds. Now, we are capable of scoring big time with our sensational laugh-doses per day.

No doubts. Begone, any personal need to waver or hesitate. I began again— a free spirit dance with my smiles and enthusiastic claps with my inner rhythm.

I was smitten, then and now...

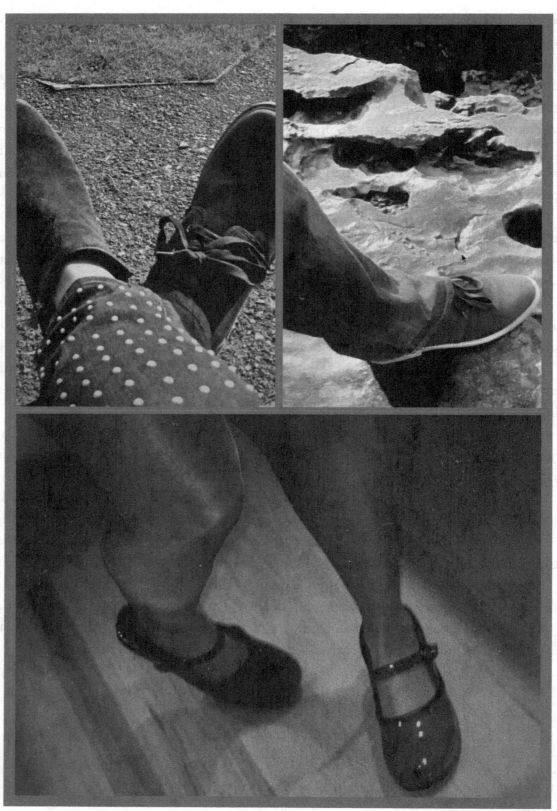

Permit the fun-filled and creative minutes to nourish our happy soul…

Sound bites

~ ~ Within the whispering winds of time, each of us chooses to
express genuine intentions to live, not just exist. We discover and
commit to the joyous seconds on our lifetime journey~ ~

~ ~Voila` There is a purposeful dismissal of any self-sabotage.
Surrender and accept become our realities. We permit the fun-
filled morsels to nourish our soul to completion~ ~

~ ~Let days, weeks, months, and years inflate the exquisite minutes for our playtime.
Breathe that essence of refreshing and rejuvenating air. Bask in the sun-kissed light~ ~

~ ~Develop playtime antennas to scout out the best treasure chests of fun.
Begin to build that trust fund for a golden aura and our playful spirit~ ~

~ ~Seek the wiser heart of frivolous jubilee. Let our heart valves open. Fine
tune our playful instruments of joy, giggles, self-love, and self-care~ ~

~ ~Begin to snicker softly. Choose to release a few giggles. Watch our tummy move in
and out rhythmically. Manifest the positive "vibes" traveling to our grateFULL heart~ ~

The High-Steppers

Friends and strangers sojourn with the historic parades and jubilant events,
Entrusting a legacy of their child-like spunk and heartfelt resolve,
Choosing to bequeath a wealth of a genial adoration, utmost joy, and indulgent glee to the world…

I am a diehard when it comes to relaxation, indulgence, and pleasure. My close friends and I put out the intention that our glass is half-full or overflowing, never half-empty.

Our global pandemic heightened a different awareness, like it or not. Many of us endorsed that the paths for better health and our emotional sustenance were vital for a life balance. My close friends and I decided to search for the welcome respites and the lighter, lively moments.

If our vote was already cast with an emphatic "let's do it," whenever the lighter times in life came forth, then our endorphins began to overflow. Our consistent commitment and partaking of our lighter fares assured an enlightening and priceless gift of our healthier, longer lifespan.

I remained a diehard in avid pursuit—whenever and wherever the lighter times sprang up. My zesty "go for it" attitude often kicked in and enhanced the invigorating options like our re-opened, outdoor events.

A nearby town was not cancelling an outdoor event during our second year of COVID. I was game to enjoy an outdoor July 4th parade, particularly when the spirited horses came into view.

There were the proud walkers, splendid trotters, and the exquisite high-steppers. They passed the people who sat, jumped up to see, or changed ASAP to the stellar viewing-positions along the colorful sidewalks.

One of the exquisite high-steppers lifted its tail to show off more than its proud pedigree. OMG, here they came—the gargantuan, pungent plops.

"Ick! Yikes. Oh, no!"

"Ohhh, look out! Is that beautiful horse gonna poop? Even while prancing along?"

"Man, that's gross."

These outcries from several children and youth came simultaneously. Their immediate nose-holds, contorted faces, and the speedy turnabouts to find giggling companions happened nonstop.

This July 4th parade provided a health bonus for any onlooker. Most of us were rapidly approaching the 145 times per day with our hysterics. Our laughs, giggles, and raucous chuckles? A guaranteed immune boost for the children, youth, parents, and even the young elders.

There was no rush or any desire to stop the out-of-control amusements for all ages. Next must-do at today's jovial venue? Just keep gawking for something else to guarantee that our tummies received the best-ever, exotic, and aerobic workout.

A street cleaner followed the horses, supposedly on behalf of the forthcoming participants in the parade. There were marching bands, enthused folks representing organizations or supporting businesses, and hand-waving drivers in classico cars. Hey, what about those gargantuan plops that awaited their arrival?

Yep, they were flattened, only removed partially by the street cleaner. Our happy, overworked tummy muscles became a foreshadowing of the nasty things to come.

"Gross. Look, they're still there!"

"Whoa! Someone is gonna step in that shit."

"Ooooooooo! Yikes!"

Well, our groupies— engaged children, youth, and several adults—gawked and grimaced as our laugh-meters tallied the ramped-up and joyous cha-chings. We clamored, as our anticipation of the next amusements soared outrageously.

Indeed, the next band members did intriguing sidesteps to stay in any semblance of a proper formation. Their inventive talents tickled our funny bones.

There were our inevitable hysterics, as the intermittent rain created a soupy, aromatic roadway. Whoa, the air waves stunk!

The children and youth loved this hoopla. There were no castaways for them.

"What *next?*"

"I wanna see *more* parade!"

"Take pictures! No, take VIDEOS to share. Did ya get that awesome guy on stilts?" Hands covered gaping mouths and the bulging eyeballs. There were crinkled or pinched noses with the turning-toxic aroma. No bewilderment why the children's and teen's remarks or antics received no adult reprimands. The incessant giggles, unforgettable faces, and witty commentaries ramped up during that spectacular day.

In hindsight, my nostrils still flared with that pungent aroma of fresh horse dung. My ears still heard the "icky" and "gross" outbursts. My eyes still saw a crowd's applause accompanying "the horses are coming!" and the animated expressions for the unsuspecting participants following that flawless (sic) street cleaner.

Snooping for our personal scorecards? Nope! We adults whizzed past the 145 times without any score cards. Alas, the effortless funnies for our laugh meter came forth naturally.

That parade was just the beginning of our holiday weekend. By the time I told my family, friends, and attended the eve fireworks, I topped the Guinness Book of world records.

My unbiased opinion? Darn close to 300 laughs. I twinkled and smirked, as I recaptured and wrote this happy-happy story.

For myself, there was a fervent promise beyond the credible research. Keep trying! Recapture any lost-and-found laughter, particularly in our "new normal" world. My high-stepper story remained pure bliss.

Side-splitting, uproarious images of those exquisite "high-stepping" horses and the lively participants in that July 4th parade were forever. The summer of 2021 and 2022 became an endowment for our world. We attended our appealing, outdoor events that were cancelled for two years.

Individuals, friends, and families opted to pursue different ways to experience their light-filled reprieves. Kaput to less angst and the incessant worries. Strengthening our confidence and contagious laughter were making a welcome comeback.

Plan A, Plan B

A whimsical and sprightly wayfaring on our discovery missions,
A unique sanctuary with their random acts of kindness and the aftermath of an inner quietude,
Acceptance of this conjoined outreach from upbeat, helpful, and gratified human beings...

Our mission was simple, according to the laugh gurus and guruettes who knew what worked in our favor. Many of us needed to keep the lost-and-found humor—yesterday, today, and tomorrow—on our front burner.

It made an enormous difference to wake up with a grin-win attitude. When our bodacious plans were dashed or kept altering, it was high time to embrace the opportunity to grin-win. Opportunity became a relief valve which "our bods" appreciated more than we suspected.

Have you moved? Made the Plan A? Made the Plan B? Perhaps, you were just winging it. When my across-the-USA move happened, I decided to create at least two plans, but they were not flushed out.

Plan A: Transform into a whirling dervish to purchase a house or condo in the touted buyer's market. Across a few months, I backed off. My initial adrenaline rush on that big investment could and should not be made hastily. Well, at least I reaffirmed one comfort. The market was changing (still is). So onward, I trekked.

Plan B: Rent a small house or condo in similar towns as my find-and-buy, adrenaline rush mission. Partake of a turtle-like pace and lighten up. Pay heed to the lightning-bolt zaps versus my light-bulb flickering—any of my duh or half-baked moments.

Perhaps, you recalled these experiences as the crystal moments when "OH, got it!" zapped you or finally arrived. Perhaps, there was a premonition, intuition or gut feeling, and a sixth sense about what to do.

My bottom line? Simplify the plans, PJ.

Plan A: First and foremost, lighten up! Plan B: Accept and know that laughter and the funnies were the real deal.

Given the mind-boggling challenges or constant worries with most moving plans, were any of us fast-forwarding our hilarious outlook and experiences? Well, I was definitely game.

I began to envision Town Halls as the place to unearth the inside scoop. You know, that town's bragging rights that I had missed due to my frantic pace. Kindred spirits went way out of their way to get me up to speed. Was that providence, marvelous karma, or good luck?

I bet that all three charms were happening. Out I pranced, literally and joyously. I grinned like an enamored kiddo, swinging their welcome bags with my sneak previews.

One favorite day included a Town Clerk who sketched on scrap paper. Presto—she gave me a treasure map to nearby condos and the town homes.

I responded with enthusiasm and a gargantuan smile. "You truly made my day with this treasure map!"

Her eyes twinkled when she stared over purple reading glasses, but she maintained a poker face. "Watch out. I'll put you to work, if you move here."

Like other clerks, she was ready to share this town's claim to fame. Her eyes twinkled again. She gestured graciously to an attractive elderly woman who entered the main office briskly.

I must digress. Did I write elderly woman? She was a far cry from any melt down in the golden years.

The clerk's smile reappeared. She gestured again to the young-at-heart elder.

"She's been volunteering ever since she retired from her town job." She continued with a soft chuckle, "That was about twenty years ago."

Both of us snatched refreshing, light-hearted minutes to enjoy the mutual soft chuckles. As I departed, imagine the bystanders that did those what-is-she-thinking stares?

A Garfield-style grin was stuck on my happy face. Man, I was on a roll and inspired with my new plans to lighten up and go with the flow.

Packets and welcomes at other Town Halls added a special sprinkling of good will and chuckles to my weekly mega-searches. I was grateful that town personnel were indulgent, since I was out to lunch about these matters in each community.

Be serious or be out to lunch, snicker, cajole, and enjoy? My continuous vote for the comic reliefs was a no-brainer. "Toto, I am *not* in Kansas any more..." was becoming my weekly mantra.

Several personnel in each town added personal tidbits, the secrets that might clench my decision to live in their "special community." The whole shebang made it easier and fun to decide where to live, definitely the nicer problem to own.

My Garfield-style smile and soft giggles reappeared, especially whenever I relived the scenarios. Our mammoth grins are often a precursor to the superb chuckles and a guarantee to raise our bar.

By George, I claimed ownership of my best pursuit. I bid a fond adieu and my good riddance of any angst or pressures about moving.

Meanwhile, that lowly statistic of four times per day for our adult amusements and frivolity? Hightail it. Skiddoo. Begone.

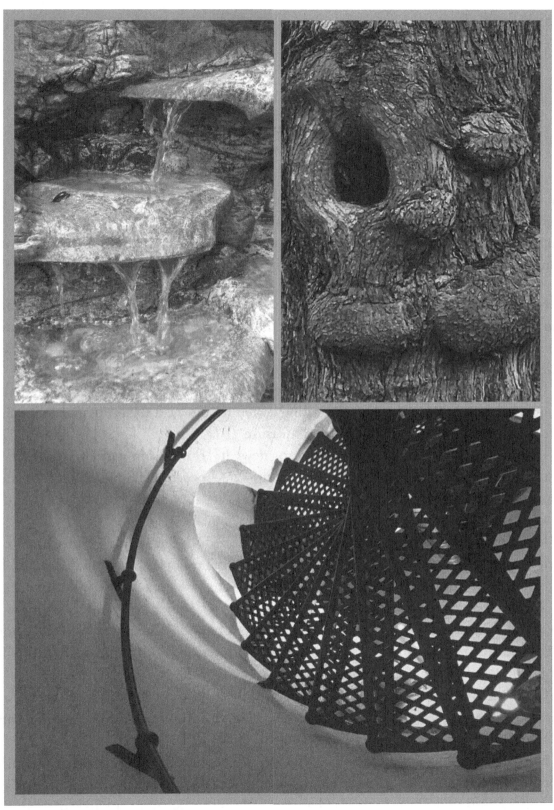

High-tail it. Skidoo. Begone. Bid a fond adieu to our angst or worrisome thoughts…

Attitude = Altitude

Choose to pursue and remain a jovial junkie,
Recreate the whimsical animal tales that transform into a welcome release,
Laughter remains a good-faith choice, reducing the beastly cortisol and inflating our robust, lively endorphins…

Ever notice that when you laugh crazily or passionately, it is a tad challenging to catch your breath? No reason for any panic attack tout the researchers. Our respiratory system is just paying close attention and adores our strenuous workout. Vamoose to our nasty cortisol is no joke. Instead, our healthy endorphins work in our favor.

Lightening the load for a few days or even weeks is transformative. Releasing balky, antagonistic stressors becomes a loving-kind action for our next scenarios and well being. Our health catapults to a wealth beyond measure.

During our global pandemic with breaking news and the latest mutations, it is beneficial to stay healthy—for our mind, body, and spirit. We choose, learn, and accommodate to defuse the teeming worries, the global angst, and our abounding stressors on any day, week, or month.

Laughter is a satisfying and good-faith choice to reduce the beastly cortisol and bring forth our robust, lively endorphins. In hindsight, my humorous remembrances and my recreation of whimsical animal stories transformed into a welcome and significant release.

When I revived my horse tales, one of my sisters was quick to interject, jesting with a witty commentary. "Why, you even *acted* like a horse! Remember? You are a horse whisperer. But, a wild-woman, animal whisperer!" she teased. Both of us ended up holding our jiggling and jouncing tummies.

Catching our breaths between my fiery recollections, my impassioned antics, and shared laughter became my A + rejuvenation. Plus, there was an advantage and a super boon for my two sisters, parents, and myself.

My parents indulged us, especially in the ways that counted. They listened to our quirky adorations—the early signs of creativity— during our childhood, crazed adolescence, and our entire adulthood. Even in their elder years, my parents loved to enhance our funniest anecdotes, amidst their breathy laughs, tummy holds, and joyful, teary eyes.

Sure, I was biased. Yet, I affirmed the terrific vibes—then and now. Amazingly, it was those body vibes and our mystical, masterful physiology that brought forth our grandiose endorphins.

These personal recreations recycled a better life balance during our global pandemic. Plus, there was another release of the notorious sibling stuff. I was pretty certain that several readers would identify and be head-nodding.

Indeed, this let-go process was a distinctive release, an authentic boost, and a flourishing reprieve for our mind, body, and spirit. Today's recreation of a wacky animal story (or other funnies) produced a sought-after place for us to lighten up.

Quite a few of my wacky horse stories were legendary. Hmmm, I was a legend in my own mind. Yeah, there was my avid pursuit of that wistful nostalgia for a few decades. There was still a vivid imagery of my speedy bike rides to a neighbor's barn.

I inherited the fine fortune to ride Vickie Gale, my neighbor's high-tone pedigree and quirky mare. She was bred to renowned stallions, but was not a brood mare. Each foal inherited an array of the acclaimed genes from the prized stallions.

Indeed, my mare's quirkiness was also one of the inherited traits. Imagine the tempting distractions and my ever-present entertainment.

One colt was a chestnut beauty with white etchings on his hind legs. His stunning, copper-gold mane and gold forelock glowed in the sunlight. As a youngster, I imagined that they glowed in the mystical veils of each evening.

Today's memorabilia for my family and close friends personified his *horsey attitude* on any day of the week. Feel free to revive the stashed memories. Our fun, lively attitudes— befriending these animals and our fellow earthlings— boosted our altitude.

This colt's *horsey attitude* became a trademark as a foal, a yearling, and even as a grown gelding. He would stare down whoever was walking by his stall. Or while he stood in the breezeway leading to a picturesque pasture.

The staring contests enticed his trademark: twitching horse lips followed by a full-fledged, turned up muzzle, as high as horsely possible. Big teeth! A lot of gum. Capture this side-splitting, amusing picture in your mind's eye.

I savored these crazed antics. I revered his horse psyche: "I can and I will. Big teeth are now laughing at you!" As an adult, I got psyched with today's animated tale.

Envision my clowning around, a minute of theatrical debut for whatever audience. I pulled and twisted my upper lip to show lotsa gum and my magnifico dental crowns at this age of my resurrected, performing arts.

The ruckus, the hilarity, and holding my stomach because it hurt so good were today's mainstays. Another certainty? Back yonder, this horse's antics were always applauded by whoever was watching his fun-frolicking, rock 'n roll times.

What a blast it was during my youth to encourage his clowning around. It unleashed a momentary nirvana from any frenzied, worldly pace.

The deja`vu nirvana returned with today's recreations. My audience of family and friends was undeniably game. Now, my boldness included my new acquaintances.

Why not recreate our playtime? Why not sustain these purposeful playtimes during our challenging, global pandemic? Adult playtime ensured that we whizzed past the lowly average of four laughs towards the mind-blowing doses of 145 times per day. We were worthy and deserving of this rejuvenating life balance.

Nowadays, I voted to remain a jovial junkie. Today's healers supported how the "funnies" positively affected our mind, heart, and soul. How nice it felt to make no excuses. No worries that my adrenaline rushes to spot other quirky horses or animals with an attitude were growing exponentially.

New comic reliefs arrived. Hurrah, our irresistible opportunities. Our daily bonus of coming closer or surpassing the once illusive 145 times for adult amusements was eminent and revered. Goodbye to any hush-hush mindsets and the rigid impositions of societal, adult-like behavior.

Enlightened mindsets and the adoption of lively attitudes and antics were finally on the front burner. Transformed adults voted by a landslide.

Enough adults chose to remain smitten and committed to share their wacky tales and humorous renewals. Bravissimo!

Wicked Good Delights

Researchers are serious when they inquire about our friends that we select for a playtime. Ever wonder why these professionals are inquisitive, deliberate, or even a bit snoopy?

These accomplished professionals recommend that we hang tight with a person or the individuals who partake of the amusements. They emphasize that children are not the only humans who are on the cutting edge. Adults own a talent to engage in the stupendous and voluminous playtimes as well.

Our playtime is relevant and worthwhile. The "now" is a perfect time for adults to create a special space. Perhaps, there is a replay of our festive memories, so we do not abandon these moments and forego that golden abundance.

Remember a neighborhood party or even a recent celebration. Did you play the game that I nicknamed, "wicked good delights?" My celebration was a recent one with a notorious partner in crime. Whimsical friends confessed to a similar scenario. Our recollections were loco and vibrant.

The partner in crime (a.k.a. your pal, sister, brother, or significant other) is across the room, pool, deck, or wherever. He or she is highly dedicated to remain in close proximity and play this inviting game of wicked good delights—without becoming the culprit.

Your role is to engage in conversations at the festive gathering. Your partner in crime makes the weirdo faces and the nonverbal signs which are undetected or stopped ASAP, if warranted.

There are higher expectations. While playing this fun game, it is mandatory to remain a cool cat, as if nothing is happening. Perhaps, there are a few dubious moments.

Try to avoid busting loose at the seams. Try not to loose control at inappropriate moments during the conversations with the other party folks. Or perhaps, something else? The whoops, crazed laughter happens at the wrong time.

I recalled my recent scene magnificently. The once-happy campers that were conversing were convinced. I was totally mad. Their stealthy or polite ways of disappearing suddenly were my partner in crime's personal gloat and glory—only from across the room. Recall what happened next with the scenario?

Most likely, a smug partner remained in his or her "safety zone." You occupied the potential "gotcha zone," trying diligently to regain a facade, an unruffled composure for the next party folks who stopped to talk. For a split second was there a wish or hope for something else?

Surely, there would be a fair chance to return the good deed (sic), putting this partner in crime in the limelight. Hopefully, a perfect moment happened during this shindig.

Hmm, might not occur. No guarantees with these games of wicked good delights.

According to my recent recollections, these adult-child playtimes are definitely loco to "pull off." Hey, the researchers stretch the limits when they endorse our laughing for no reason. They support the ultimate proof that our healthy belly laughs feel grandiose, leading to outlandish, comical hysterics.

What better reason to entice our childish ear-to-ear grins? Our game of partners in crime means be ready at any time or place to show our moxie, the rapture, and a contagious glee. Researchers nudge us to behold how the folks at a festive celebration smile, chuckle, or crack up with our antics.

Any repetition with this game of wicked good delights underscores a mutual adult-child craving to pursue the dynamic duo playtimes. Alas, one person is in the "safety zone." Undoubtedly, the partner is in "the limelight."

Our clowning around is absolute ecstasy, as we quickly approach the children's 145 giggle-times per day. We do not want to overlook the additional and valuable bonus. It is a blast to partake and enjoy our suspense-filled playtime.

Credible researchers endorse that our style of laughter, the what-makes-us-laugh-so-hard syndrome, is a superb medicine. Contemporary sitcoms, irresistible jokes or cartoons, and the humorous downloads on our techno-gadgets fit the bill as well.

Each time-out becomes the soulful elixir and a super charger for any of us in the grand scheme of our day-to-day living. During our global pandemic and current or projected mutations, the undulating scenarios remain unsettling. The diverse relief valves and our creative playtime, like the whimsical partners in crime, remain the priceless gifts.

We vote to surrender these ongoing stressors. Indulge in the high jinks, like the comical partners in crime. Partake of our merriment. No guilt-trips about our inner child and these playful time-outs. Our mind, body, and spirit remain happily in sync.

There is no mystique while playing this game of delights, particularly as the adult kiddos. Partners in crime rarely squelch or ignore their mutual desires. Instead, their avid pursuits of the wicked good delights at festive gatherings or a recent jubilee are envied.

Signs of a Truce

Coax and seize a "fixer-upper" on each day,
Delight with an overload of intoxicating funnies,
Accept and sustain the memorable minutes, hours, or a day…

Abandon, discard, or set free our humdrum funk. Favor and accept the choice to alter an uninspired day or our lackluster week. Observe, keep watching, and hang loose for the diversions and our joyful bliss.

Researchers keep on top of the latest scoop. They endorse us glancing in a mirror and starting our day with an expression of self-love and a smile. Throughout the day, they encourage us to keep googling for a seductive, bewitching opportunity and head straight for our spasmodic, zany giggles. P.S. These healthier pursuits are a genuine claim to fame.

Certain moments manifest a first-class guarantee, bringing forth our flourishing sense of humor. Vamoose—to our distress, the leftover angst, a surge of apprehension, or any negative vibrations.

Personally, I adopted this search-and-find mission on several days, weeks, and months. I elected to watch mindfully. There was a rediscovery of the enticements. Our entertainment with the slapstick or comical signs happened, especially in certain places.

Where art thou? One fine locale is the animal kingdom. Unconditional caring tends to coexist, rather nicely for us humans, afforded these opportune moments.

It is true. A few dogs and cats are not the best buddies. Then how do these critters that are not the best pals manage to ferret out and catch a mystical "harmonic" balance?

I watched intently. Avoidance or harassment of each other dominated until a curiosity, a boldness, a lightening bolt, or you name it took over. It appeared to be anybody's guess as to which species risked—that first dare, the incredible taunting, or a gargantuan provocation.

The initial appearance of tolerance between these dogs and cats rarely translated to "I like you now." Another truth? "Adore" was definitely overboard.

The next scuffles and amusing territorial rituals were fair game. In another week or month (who kept count) that same dog and cat were now friends, even sleeping in close proximity.

The next miracles of closeness and fewer spats in the critter attack zones happened. At obvious moments, there was an impulsive or cocky sampling of each other's food, without the undue harassments.

These nose-to-nose communiqués tickled our funny bones. C'mon, I was not the only former owner or a wanton observer who became infatuated and treated to the amusing signs of a truce. The eminent and elevated hysteria tallied up our fabulous score.

We adults squelched our bad statistic of only four times per day for our tee-heeing. By now, we adult-kiddos were on a definite lookout for another "fix" of that unrivaled fire in our bellies.

It was also marvelous to backtrack, especially when we decided to up the ante for today's giggles. Images of my former German shepherd "Beau" and our cat "Butchie-e-e" recharged my beloved sense of humor. Beau and Butchie-e-e swapped amazing traits that were uncharacteristic and definitely unbecoming of their pedigree.

Any naysayers out yonder? Well, my Beau and Butchie-e-e attained that critter tranquility, that mystical "harmonic" balance. They snoozed together with ludicrous postures, eventually adopting one another's fun antics by osmosis (sic). They were the smashing pals that remained my enticements, even for today's daily fix.

I was betting the ranch on it, although I did not own a ranch…yet. Several of us adults, not just these priceless critters, were ready to commit to a daily fix.

Feel free to recollect the different animal buddies and those amusing signs of a truce. Inevitably, most adults paused longer to recall an urgency for the feel-good moments with the cackles. We knew the researchers were applauding, especially with our healthier endeavors.

Committed adults reflected about something equally as good for our psyches. Saying "adios" to the daily minutia, the "wee" stuff that never mattered. We yearned to take a super break from the worldly undulations and our next mutations. Alive and committed, we bragged and nodded with the notorious grins.

Perhaps, our constant lookout for the dog-cat phenomenon was like tuning into a favorite sitcom. As today's appreciative audience, it was a hoot to be privy to the critter-comedy hour. The dog-cat antics, fun signs of a truce, and the heavenly bliss kept us connected in the best ways.

It was not rocket science. Enough adults craved the highest doses of amusement. Intrigued adults dared to change their giggle-probability on any day or week.

Why not? Our go-for-it motto was an elixir for our better health and well being. Children and youth often appreciated our wake-up momentum.

We kept our eyes wide open and relished this joy of being bug-eyed. Then we became the noticeable diehards, always on stand by. We chose purposefully—to whoop it up with our feisty attitudes and our gales of laughter.

Recall our animal buddies and the amusing signs of a truce or how
easily *one* animal-friend becomes our daily sitcom…

Sound bites

~ ~Climb the ladder rungs to discover new venues of buoyant play.
Become a caregiver and caretaker of these unexpected playtimes~ ~

~ ~Commit to refresh the playtime energy. Explore freely to raise the bar for laughter~ ~

~ ~Nurture a happy state of the soul. Enjoy the detours,
pathfinding, and the regal vistas~ ~

~ ~When a lack-luster of silly is present, infuse a search-and-
find mission with memorable tidbits of wit and charm~ ~

~ ~Dissolve into play games with a harmonica, a crescent moon,
bubbles, soft sand-toe artistry, and festive sparklers~ ~

~ ~Transform your worries into a mellow state of mind. Begin to move forward with a
peaceful smile. Feel your shoulders lift from any mind-chatter remnants and stress~ ~

Mama Stealth, Let's Ride!

Witness the mystique of Mother Nature or the idyllic, nostalgic venues like a miraculous looking-glass,
Surrender to the forthcoming rapture, a receptive heart, and a virtuous soul,
Lighten up and permit any remnants of human adversity to diminish as an adult-kiddo emerges…

Humor primes an optimistic attitude. Attitude boosts our altitude. Many of us start with a smile and graduate to a few chuckles. Pretty soon, the boisterous laughs monopolize certain moments that we experience on an unforgettable day or a remarkable week.

Were we on the same page of the playbook with a vivid recollection? For me, it was an idyllic day. Suddenly, I felt an inspirational attitude propelling a dynamic surge in my personal altitude.

A definite boost in my altitude happened whenever I took an adventuresome spin in my different vehicles. "Let's Ride!" was my intentional self-prompt to trigger another merry escapade.

My pick-up, a daily pick-me-up in the rain and the sunshine, was Mama Stealth. Former trucks of equal repute were Stealth Rod, Brandywine, and Bubbette. I did own Azul, one of the Vega hatchbacks of the 1970s. All of those vehicles were destined for the mini or maxi-adventures. This time was no exception.

"Let's ride," I exclaimed with enthusiasm, as I sprinted towards Mama Stealth. I relished talking to my beloved vehicles. "Indeed, it is high time, Mama Stealth!"

My adult-kiddo was on a roll, darn ready to adventure. Revisit a cherished childhood and youthful reprieve. Head towards the Charles River through the towns west of Boston. Good thing for autopilot, that gotta-take-over-for-PJ phenomenon.

I was in another zone, daydreaming and visualizing the rapture of that afternoon. The Charles River would be rushing over the dam in a quaint town. The locale was a pit stop for the bicyclers. Occasionally, the outdoorsy adults, teens, and children walked or jogged there. This pit stop became my oasis that was rarely crowded.

I envisioned sitting near the churning falls in the glowing sunlight, writing, and savoring the splendid day. I would stroll along either side of the Charles River that flowed around a small island below the dam.

This particular day? Earth to PJ… Somehow, I managed to travel to my destination without a fender-bender. Hmm, it was a foreshadowing of things to come.

Before I arrived at my envisioned reprieve, I made a left turn, not a right turn. For a split second, I was semi-dazed. Thank goodness for my beam-me-up daydreams.

Meanwhile, Mama Stealth's auto-pilot had no "duh" moments. Head to the farm about a mile from my original destination. Recapture my nostalgic child and youthful memories: the smell of fresh hay bales, molasses oats, and aromatic shavings in the stalls.

Wow, I was reliving a super-charge of my youth: live to ride, ride to live. Stay in my saddle to jump my pokey or my feisty horses in that towering, gray barn.

Ha! I adored these horseback riding lessons far better than the piano lessons. My parents accepted my deal of fewer years than my two sisters who adored the twinkling ivories on our piano. More expensive for my horse playtime, but I was smitten with those mares, geldings, and foals in that towering, gray barn.

My sister half-joked, "You *are* a horse!" Later in life she added, "You have a beautiful horse soul. You are an animal whisperer. Let's look up horses in my animal totem book."

Back to today's fun adventure… Mama Stealth was still on autopilot (sic). It was mind-blowing how my "let's ride" enticed such a rejuvenation and my effortless grins. I would have been at the Charles River, but this nostalgic destination became today's cha-ching for my laugh meter.

Today's barn? My gargantuan barn with cherished horses was no longer there. However, the vintage farm stand was upscale and "go green" in its appeal. I did spot a smaller red barn, undoubtedly a downsized version of my reminisces.

An inner urge lured me to that smaller red barn. I went with today's flow, following the arrows and signs that revealed a petting zoo. The adult-kiddos were equally welcome.

On this gifted day, there was a couple with curious youngsters. All of us engaged readily in the human-critter playtime.

My unbiased estimation? Both the children and we adults zoomed towards the 145 daily laughs.

The young children's attention span went defunct. Not so for my attention span. I was primed to snatch my exclusive time.

Happy snorts from the massive pigs Romeo and Juliet were keepsakes. Several goats with stances on corral doors to greet me and munch on my long locks were comical appeals. The ecstasy and synchronicity were addictive.

My adult-kiddo was let loose again. I found playmates (a ditto for the playful animals). I decided to zoom back to the Charles River for a nostalgic peek, but the sunshine enticed a different summons for Mama Stealth and myself. Head to a different nostalgic reprieve.

The late afternoon and wind gusts brought out the braver souls. A visitor center with whimsical crafts and gifts became a welcome refuge. It was tended by a woman who expected the family critters and the braver earthlings to arrive.

"I make sure to keep lots of treats," she remarked with a chuckle, while pointing to the foyer. Two dogs scarfed up her goodies and slurped water from her whimsical bowls. Meanwhile, we adults enjoyed her munchies placed on quirky plates to insure our giggle-meter worked overtime. I adored our feel-great, buoyant spirits.

I was hooked. My adult playtime took over with my "let's ride" afternoon. I headed back to Mama Stealth, smitten with the ripple effects of today's adventures.

Nothing like reminisces, moments left unplanned, and the grins that deepened the smile lines on my face. I remembered what else happened during my free-wheeling, let's ride adventures.

My feisty spirit emerged. Good riddance to the grim "adult" statistics and hello to the easy 145-plus laughs per day. I continued my bliss, as I patted Mama Stealth's dashboard affectionately and spoke enthusiastically to her.

"Native Americans and the ancient Greeks knew the healing effects of this bliss, way ahead of their time. Why not indulge our healing spirit?" Mama Stealth and I did not forget.

"Mama Stealth, let's ride!" I laughed softly, patted her dashboard, and smirked all the way home.

Another stellar manifestation for that day came forth, as I parked my treasured Mama Stealth. I spoke aloud with a confident pizzaz and my loving-kind pats to the dashboard.

"Absolutely! Attitude = Altitude!"

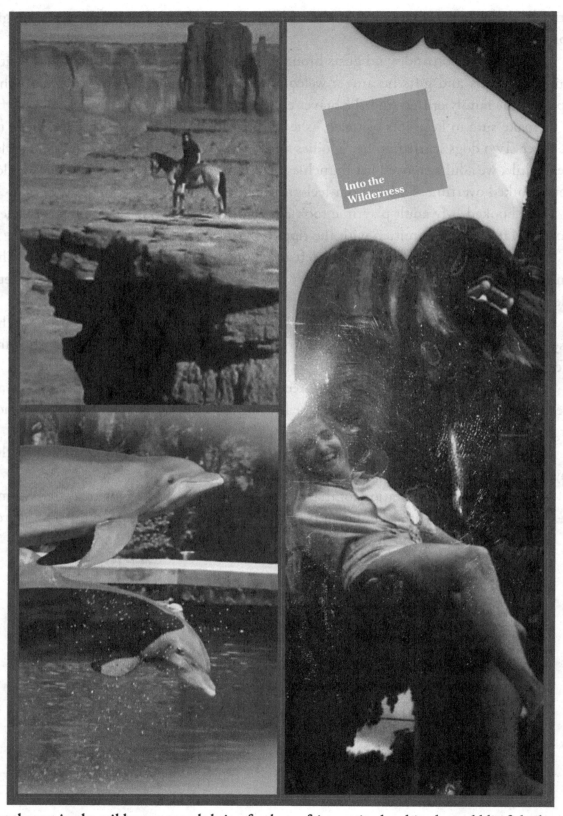

Into the Wilderness

Let the out-in-the-wilderness travels bring forth our feisty attitude, altitude, and blissful vibes...

Ramp Up The Tempo

Aim for a higher count of laugh-doses each day,
Peals of laughter create an authentic cha-ching for our laugh meter,
Envision a blast from the past, a frolicking time and locale with the natural delights…

Anybody recollecting the 1970s? My hippy Woodstock memorabilia and stream of today's storytelling ramped up the tempo for my friends and myself. We recounted our nostalgia and admitted to the amusing anecdotes about our tie-dyed attire, the deafening rock music, soulful folk singers, and an entertaining barrage of mega-leftovers.

Other ramped-up tempos happened in the early 1970s. I hooked up with an educational theatre troupe traveling throughout New Hampshire. Our hippy van was blazing red with its artistic design of flowers and free spirit. Hmm, the New Hampshire "live free or die" license plate was a statewide, no-tolls plate.

"Wassup with this *state* vehicle?" a few inquisitive or semi-sarcastic people would ask. That question was rather mild.

Imagine the other inquisitions. The human, piranha-feeding frenzy was inevitable. "Who are YOU?"

"What would you be doing for the *state* of New Hampshire?"

"How do you get away with a no-tolls plate in a hippy van? Can I ride with ya?"

Yeah, we were stopped. The blazing-blue lights and blaring sirens appeared way more than a few times. Oh, very suspicious! A *state* vehicle?

The artsy designs and the fine print of our university on the side triggered the Q & A moments with the police. Rural or urban locales commanded that equal and immediate attention.

Life was still good. There were the hoots, plentiful hollers, avid journalists, and our eager crowds. Guess how our creative performances with children in rural, suburban, or urban areas faired?

Wunderbar! Astounding photos accompanied the front-page stories and our television coverage. The grandiose crowds dazzled the town residents and even our theatre troupe.

Our reputation began to spread quickly, oftentimes before our next stint. To say our trio was highly challenged with rambunctious children and awesome youth overeager to participate was an understatement.

Alas, there was no puzzlement. We needed to add a tidbit (sic) of the child-control theatrics to our shindigs of creative dramatics, participative puppetry, sing-a-longs, and whatever else that we improvised.

My "Little Red Wagon" scrapbook included the news releases that revealed this unbridled enthusiasm. Fun-filled photos accompanied the front-page stories throughout the state. It was impossible to miss the children's exuberant faces and open-mouthed hysteria in color print and the "gotcha" faces of our tour troupe. Never say never…

Today, the finest doctors and holistic healers would be applauding that our theatre troupe went for a super immersion to learn with the children's glee and laughter. They would encourage us to celebrate the spontaneity—to guarantee our untapped amusements.

Our employers teased and supported us. "Man, you guys! You are the young kiddos at play. We just might show up at a festive gig!" Well, how about my readers, right in this exact moment?

Are you enjoying a "blast from your past," envisioning a frolicking time with the natural delights? What a far cry from any boring or yucky summer jobs that I survived while earning monies toward my college tuition.

I loved these experiences so much that the "Little Blue Wagon" became my first business venture. I became the owner, director, actress, manager, financial wizard, and a very smitten adult-kiddo. Little did I know.

I was also a co-writer with my two employees and a carpenter-painter for our semi-ingenious, portable stage and puppet theatre. Both portables were cinched on top of an old, high-mileage car. Our high-jinks playtime began and continued in my welcoming state of Massachusetts.

As one of the painters of our art for children on my best friend's old and high-mileage car, I was reminded daily. Family and our close friends guessed correctly—what he dared to say.

"You owe me BIG time!" Then my best buddy and I cracked up and hugged. After our summer joys, he returned to the University of Massachusetts with his colorful, cutesy car. This auto was his only transportation forever, so he proclaimed at the time.

Of course, his college classmates caught sight of our "Little Blue Wagon" tooling around campus for his collegiate years. "Invisible" happened only in his wildest dreams. His friends made up a multitude of whimsical, fantasized stories.

I confess. I still owe him BIG time.

I shared these keepsakes for years. People responded pronto.

"I love to be around children. They are free, so uninhibited."

"Children make us less inhibited. We even begin to regress! It is a healthy regression."

"Did you know what I read about a year ago? Adults need to laugh more. I think I am watching children more than ever."

Hey, these folks already knew the research. Perhaps, they heard a few sound bites about our misplaced, funny side of living for adults.

Do we adults really want to sulk and hang tight to the dark side of living? Or do we want to entice, seize, and savor the fun episodes of living?

Most children become our super role models, whenever they laugh and tempt us. Preschoolers often giggle, especially when they misname things.

A shoe becomes a "floo." They say things like, "itsy, bitsy" or "tummy, bummy, lummy," while letting their giggle-meter soar. Engaged adults who succumb and catch their contagious giggles soar with the natural highs. Perhaps, they give the splendid high-fives as well.

We recalled being mesmerized by the lighten up feelings that surfaced with the glee and cheerful attitudes of children and witty teens. All their hoopla kick-started the creative ways to ramp up our tempo.

Of course, a big bonus was timely and appreciated. When our adult tempo quickened, we literally charged onward towards that reputable 145 laugh-doses per day.

Voila` What a piece of cake. Why hold back? Aim for a higher count of laugh-doses each *and* every day.

Our peals of laughter are an authentic cha-ching for our laugh meter. Well, if we are going to be exhausted, why not strive to become the happiest earthlings on our planet? In our vast universe?

Hooked

High-five the scenarios that trigger a pizzazz,
Stretch to invent and own a whacky psyche,
Feel an enchantment with the riveting, side-splitting hysterics…

I was hooked, searching for the chipper and frolicsome days. Such liveliness became a natural-high addiction for my superlative bragging rights. Indeed, it was appealing to snafu these jovial scenarios and my relaxing time-outs.

One rousing and guaranteed hook was my "animal appreciation" days, no matter what the season. These refreshing days promised to reactivate my good-ache, belly laughs.

Go, PJ antibodies! Go, PJ white blood cells! Such findings were touted by the brilliant scientists. These good-ache, tummy jiggles were the primo catalysts to fight off our infections and a mishmash of any creeping crudola (sic).

Get outta town? No way! I raved over the high probability and the beneficial paybacks documented by our credible professionals. Never any worries—when it came to launching the "PJ animal appreciation" days.

My intentional and hooked day happened in the winter season. An aerobatic, bushy-tailed squirrel captured my rapt attention.

This spunky squirrel zipped across my balcony ledge, soared to a cement wall below my condo, and darted across the quiet parking lot. I believed that several readers were experiencing a personal deja`vu (feel free to envision your favorite animal). Meanwhile, my fearless squirrel flaunted a fantastical savvy.

The next daring leaps came from the branches of my stately pine trees. A breathtaking flurry, a wicked-flying leap, and another snow-dusted pine tree was graced with the flawless gymnastics. These squirrelly-antics were topped off with our winter splendor and the culminating snow mists.

"Whoa down, a 10-plus!" I bellowed in awe, awarding a top-squirrelly score for an engaging performance. If my sliding patio door had been open, just imagine the happy bellowing.

Indeed, the PJ echoes of "Areeeba!" in squirrel-talk came forth. "Tarzan of yesterday, eat your heart out," I embellished. Bewitched and entranced with my gifts of hilarity became an understatement.

I clinched the quality time to pay closer attention and be entertained. Kindred souls were often hooked with their diverse "animal appreciation" days, particularly in the re-awakening spring. Today, I adored my gifted minutes to fast forward with my euphoric proclamation.

"Wunderbar! In another month, our spring arrives. A blend of our last cold and the next budding surprises are forthcoming."

This year's emergence of spring brought the unexpected warm, humid days with downpours, deafening thunder, and lightning bolts that zigzagged across the sky. Steamy vapors were rising in my back parking lot, casting a mystical spell. I was game.

The storm was quelled, according to my meteorological ESP. Inhaling deeply of the cleansing air, I smelled the fragrant begonias and a divine cedar mulch. I rounded the curve, enamored with the steamy vapors in the smaller, back parking lot. My day was transforming into a charmed evening for an inviting stroll...or so I thought.

As I meandered towards the crimson maple trees, I spotted Calico. My namesake was befitting for the cat colorings, but not very ingenious. This scurry-away cat of late winter became the hey-where-ya-been cat with our early spring. As I spoke with fetching intonations, Calico wandered my way.

Calico proceeded to sashay in and out of my long legs. Then began to nuzzle 'round and 'round my extended hand, as though it was a five-star catnip. Shortly thereafter, I was on the human prowl.

Where was an ideal branch for our lofty playtime? Calico's sharp claws and swats produced a snap, crackle, and pop, quickly altering Mother Nature's toy. The shorter branch was worthy for belly rubs and a last attack with eager forepaws, before the toy was doomed.

No worries. Rub me, love me, and I shall shed on thee took up where my toy branch left off. The playful nibbles were attempted, but were quickly nipped in the bud by myself. Piece of cake, as my ecstasy rubs were too hypnotic to bring back Calico's playful nibbles.

I hereby professed these worldly "animal appreciation" days to be mandatory for us earthlings. Playful laughs between the animal-kingdom critters and any of us enticed the famous NK. The famous NK?

Researchers predicted that these *natural killer* cells, the revered NK cells, became our best warriors and warriorettes against cancer. This newsflash affirmed my PJ be-ready motto.

I knew when my cup runneth over and rarely protested, once the revered researchers gave a constant green light. I elected to zoom by my recent "duh" or senior moments with another "animal appreciation" day and the flashbacks.

I was rarely alone. Several adults aimed for the "high fives" whenever images of their "animal appreciation" days reappeared from their short or long-term memory bank.

My visions rebounded (no hallucinations). Vivid images of the spring-loaded leaps and aftermath of snow mists created by my Tarzan-squirrel still produced the best medicine—laughter. Ditto with my cat fix. Calico understood purr-fectly about our tree-branch playtime in the company of my PJ massage-rubs.

"Then and now" mattered. Those treasured chuckles propelled me far beyond the skimpy projection for most adults.

Even without a score pad, I owned bragging rights with my top-notch, winter-spring score. With my Tarzan-squirrel and Calico cat, I whizzed by the measly four times for adults. I landed closer to the sought-after 145 laughs per day.

I focused earnestly for my world-class, primo status. I favored the yellow brick road that the professional wizards kept advocating. This magical road lead naturally to our best-ever medicine—letting go to snatch the laughter. Celebrating and enjoying the capers, antics, and incredible laughs manifested our super-elevated moods. Let 'em rip!

Perhaps, a daily ritual of "hooked" became a must-do. Perhaps, a search and this ritual morphed into an overdue rite of passage. A loving-kind manifestation emerged.

Look in the mirror and make a few faces. Guaranteed to bring on a smile, most likely a welcome chuckle. Greet the day when you go outdoors. Look at "something or someone" that entices a giggle, the frivolity, or the unforgettable entertainment and your gaiety.

Astonishment and these eureka moments inspire what our mind, body, and soul crave naturally. None of us really needs the professional nudges to realize that laughter is our best medicine.

Yay! Healthier and fun-loving indulgences create our genuine intentions and realistic manifestations. Woo-Woo! An enlightened attitude crops up. Our purposeful choice to be "hooked" entices us to shift into a higher, glorious, and a fun-loving gear.

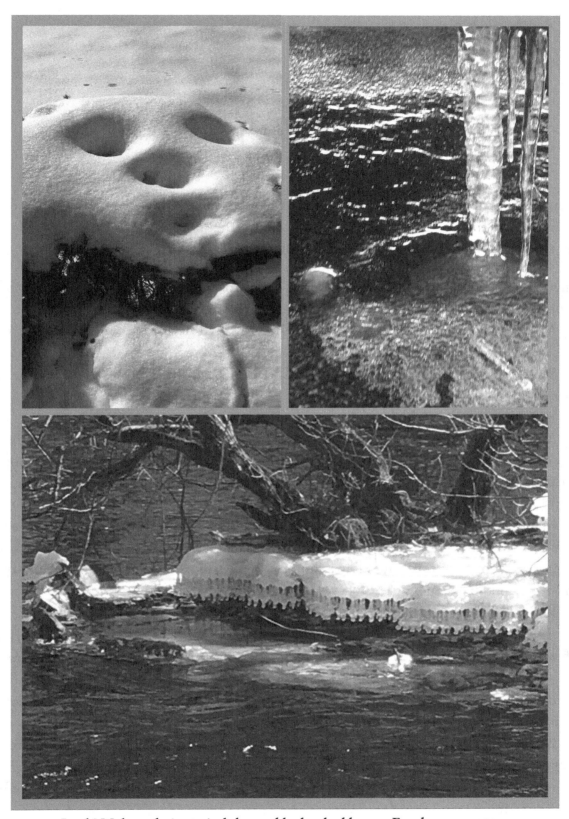

Look! Make a choice to indulge and be hooked by our Eureka moments…

Almost Looney Tunes

Charge onward with deeper inhales and exhales to visualize an inner, harmonic peace,
Summon and nod to all the gods and goddesses for the snickers to start again,
Let the almost looney tunes revolutionize a never-never land…

Anyone out there going bonkers with today's phone menus and an unfathomable number of options? Did I ask a push-the-right-button question, no pun intended?

Answers appear to be forthcoming, ONLY if… We listen to the robotic voice on exactly how to proceed *very* carefully.

Most of us are quick to mutter or sputter. The options and our attempts to communicate are not understood.

Starting over? Fuhgeddaboutit!

Ah, patience is an honorable attribute or today's understatement. The researchers endorse that we need to search harder for any amusement. However, more effort is not a reason to stop searching for the positive effects of our "funnies" during any day, week, or month.

In my back-to-sanity minutes with these notorious phone-robots, I fessed up and spewed aloud. "Tis a big Kahuna stretch to come clean on a look-harder day or week. How about my attempts to find any tidbits of humor in my wait time or during my strung-out and tricky phone menus?"

Enough is enough. Too much energy to spew aloud.

If my miraculous, semi-tolerant mood was prevalent that day, I started to notice that a few phone menus included a polite offer. "If you want to talk to a representative, please press zero." Sometimes, this helpful hint was accomplished readily by pressing one number.

If I was not paying close attention, here came my boomerang. Yep, my semi-psychotic flashbacks happened recently.

Beware, PJ! Any pleasant, never-to-be-found-again human took a tailspin into a deeper abyss. My press of an incorrect number during this phone-endurance test meant the return of you know who. My never-ever distraught, robotic voice was neither playful nor entertaining.

Yah, voodoo! Perhaps, juju was alive and well.

Fast forward. I did what the holistic healers advocated.

I paused. I took deeper, slower breaths. In hindsight, there were a few chuckles about that almighty sound bite and my shakin' loose. I began to let my laugh tallies gain momentum, in spite of the next interludes.

"I'm sorry, I did not understand," continued the ever-patient, robotic voice. "Ask me another question."

I pretended to have a semi-desperate plea. "User-friendly options where art thou?"

There was the plentiful wait-time. Professionals reminded us not to take ourselves so seriously. So… Back to my forever wait-time and Plan B. I began laughing at myself, especially as I was trying way too hard to be right or attain perfection.

I made my weirdo faces in a nearby mirror, sang off-key with the menu options, and turned up the speaker-phone. I created my free style dance, while the elevator music played and played. And, of course, played much longer.

Aha, there was such a thing as MIGHTY karma. Today, that illusive option to declare "representative or agent" was heard.

I smirked—a mini-score for my higher-humor tallies. I applauded the once-unattainable "press zero for an operator" to snatch my euphoric high with a sought-after human.

Hearing a human voice replaced my looney-tune mind chatter. During my talks with a real human being, here came something else to elicit my *crazed* laughs.

"I need to transfer you to another department for the right person."

My exasperation ramped up. "Hey, hello, hello-o-o-o?" A real human managed to cut off my important call. Now, I was "number one in the cue" with that supposed transfer to the right person.

"No-o-o-o-o-o-o-o-o-o-o-o-o-o-o-o-o-!"

What needed to happen ASAP? Really not sure in today's moment, but I was in my abode. Well, I tried out a mini-primal scream, albeit the psychological benefits of this release were touted a few decades ago.

I charged onward with my deepest inhales and exhales to visualize my inner, harmonic peace. I summoned and nodded to all the gods and goddesses for my snickers to start again.

Was there still a guarantee for laughter (crazed, sarcastic, or whatever) with this whole shebang? In the big picture--my juiciest parts of everyday life and living--this "phone stuff" was never terminal, not forever and ever.

Now was my prime time to let go. My almost looney tunes faded to a never-never land. My past minutes were already over. I began to snicker at my mini-theatre of the absurd, my melodrama that I survived with my outrageous and rather inventive breaks.

Hmm, was my transformation like the famed gurus and guruettes endorse? Was it not a liberation to affirm that our human imperfections were okay? That PJ and other earthlings were capable of laughter, even in the looney-tune moments?

Hmm, what did the gurus and guruettes recommend the *next* time? Create the ingenious, comical faces in a nearby mirror. Do massive amounts of faces. Hum a funny tune, preferably off-key. Purposefully lighten up and cut oneself a little slack. Make a promise not to "de-genius" with our abundance of phone menus.

Aim for the outrageous, slapstick humor. Try another belly dance, even to the not-so-exotic phone music. Invent different menu options that bring forth the uncontrollable giggles for a late night show. Let a free spirit soar and embellish another diversion.

Try ALL or a smidge of the fun antics while waiting. Intentionally ditch the "wee" stuff (a.k.a. phone menus) to rise above the looney-tune moments.

Please do—smug it. Notice something else?

Any of those lowly predictions of four times per day for our adult funnies already went kaput. Bypassing our "in a tizzy" or "going berserk moments" helped us to be inventive during the exasperating or our cranky minutes.

Something else was fashioned and created on our behalf. Upping our ante converted these "in a tizzy" minutes into a playful, whimsical, or an imaginative challenge.

Huzza! Rah-rah! We became clever or brilliant when we rose above and figured out another ingenious plan.

Begone, our winter doldrums or woes. Surrender to our compelling
legacy of "spring fever" and the outdoor zest...

The Diehards

Bleep out any of the winter doldrums,
Surrender to a legendary "spring fever,"
Partake of nature's mystique and an outdoor zest…

I figured my move back to New England was an entitlement to rediscover a few haunts. Beam-me-there-Scotty seemed to be out of commission, so I forged ahead.

Guess who tried to beat me to my nostalgic park beside the enchanting lake? The feisty diehards who caught IT big time.

Today was the official day. Hoorah, it was spring. Of course, we diehards caught IT—a spring fever. Mother Nature ruled the roost, ready or not. The cooler weather got our attention, as the wind gusts across the enchanting lake remained downright nippy.

Would the inevitable goose bumps and shivers send any of us diehards scurrying away? Not a chance… Besides, it was taboo for a dyed-in-the-wool zealot to cop out on the official day.

All of us would surrender to a lofty madness. Was it was an easy choice? Indeed, especially when it came down to the *official* day and catching IT (a.k.a. spring fever, a legendary outdoor mania).

We diehards stored up this anticipated spring fever during our winter doldrums. We did not forget. Our playtime with engaging howls, wild shrieks, and contagious laughs were irresistible, inescapable, and compelling.

Today's researchers, doctors, and healers reminded and prompted us to engage fully. They respected that our immune systems got a vacation from our nagging distress and worry, an authentic boost for our longevity curve.

They nudged us to move in positive directions that made a quality difference in our daily living. Even Zoom facilitators during COVID—19 and the unpredictable mutations became the constant encouragers and the empaths on our mindful journeys.

Encouragements… Be mindful of the happiness, those who brightened a particular day. Become a keen observer, the more-than-ready participant in a playtime. Brief moments? Longer timespans?

The tallies kept a-comin' in our favor. At today's lakeside, my soaring tallies with the shared smiles and laughter arrived with the refreshing, premature attacks of our spring fever.

I did not zone out and forget. Most daily hoopla was an incalculable gift, especially as all of us kept hearing the breaking newscasts about our "new normal" and the fated mutations.

Why not keep up with the positive cha-chings for our laugh meter? Just let go and visualize today's special effects with any of the premature attacks of this spring fever and our outdoor mania.

I observed another treasure trove of happiness that *official* day and during the next weeks at this enchanting lake. Our laugh meters were elevated incredibly. The 145 times per day for children was a piece of cake for us adult-kiddos. Arrivederci to our measly four times per day.

Early bird fishing techniques, chock full of the imperfections, triggered our contagious laughs. Wannabe sailing teams and the kayaking partners were relearning the trials, the tribulations, and the "new normal" park rules. Everything sparked a comic relief and the nirvana for a multitude of us adult-kiddos.

The individuals or groups on an early spring mission tromped playfully through the saturated, muddy grasslands in the nearby meadow. Whenever these walkabouts or runabouts went kaput, certain folks headed to their cars for a siesta or the witnessing of a rallying spirit.

Open car windows guaranteed the finger-pointing, louder snickers, or our sneaky photos. Individuals with cool shades posed and flaunted the grins or the spring-fever entertainment while being photographed. Videos and the creative selfies were hysterical.

Today's fanaticism and outdoor mania became epidemic, especially with the afternoon's warmer bennies. More diehards came primed for today's promise of the spring-like temperatures. They were obsessed with our golden rule to hang loose.

Basking in the divine sunshine, required by state law, attained our optimum vitamin D (sic). Going for it—the *official* spring arrival with a warmer-than-last-week temperature was seized. The spring-fever addiction was magnifico.

Do ya think that I left the park early to trade in my premature attack of spring fever for a better spring-like day? Not a chance… Today was simply the best no-brainer. Immersing in our splendor of outdoor mania was compelling.

My day morphed into the prized opportunities and the effortless bongs on my giggle-meter. I surpassed the 145 times per day for the child-like hysteria—what a piece of cake.

I sang off-key to mimic chirping birds, enjoying their "critter" bouts of spring fever. My feisty spirit attracted a seagull that kept soaring nearby. Perhaps, this seagull sensed my golden aura or checked out this big kiddo at play.

I adored the biggie-sized grins plastered on my face. My stomach craved the leftover bellyaches, as I voted to let today's good times roll.

I chuckled with a group of teens that were bedazzled by my non-stop playtime. Their afternoon antics underscored a blast from my past. They rocked their sailboats crazily and then pretended they were going to crash into other boats. Deliriously happy peers, the uninhibited children, and my happy self were rad, stupendous, and striking.

Several of the children eyeballed me. Was I game?

"Hi," I exclaimed, as I smiled at a preschooler emerging from the towering, pine-sheltered picnic area. My smiley face and waving hands got her fired up. She kept waving, stumbling, and running my way. Her mother and I watched her daughter with the ultimate amusement.

"Thank God we can get outside with COVID and the mutations. We're having yummy snacks here," she beamed, between our chuckles. Mom ventured to redirect her daughter to their festive picnic table.

Meanwhile, our laugh-meters and tallies zoomed upward with her daughter's mischievous antics. I knew the three of us were tied as far as the top notch laughs. Somehow, I managed to talk between our shared playtime and the alluring giggles.

"Isn't it an amazing day? All of us want to get outside to play, play, play!" I affirmed, with a huge grin. Her Mom agreed and kept smiling. Her daughter attained her giggles of ecstasy with a playtime of pure delight.

If laughter was touted as a longevity tonic by different professionals, why not partake? They continued to encourage us to make a daily effort on behalf of our health, well being, and the positive effects. I certainly did not forget their sage advice and their encouragements.

I was delighted to continue today's adventures and headed around the park. Another child of equal repute was not about to miss his prospects for playtime.

"Boo," he shouted, with the rat-a-tat laughs, as he clamored down the dock where I went to sit and relax. I cracked up, which he loved.

"Oh, you scared me," I exclaimed, half-pretending with a few jumps and staring at his twinkling eyes. When I pulled down my shades, he witnessed my twinkling eyes and knew. My belly laughs erupted as he crept around my back, ready to pull off another funny marathon.

"Are you gonna scare me again?" I teased, thinking that he would dare.

"Nope!" But, he continued along the dock, laid down, and pretended to be a surfer. His marathon playtime was super—undoubtedly his claim to fame that day.

"Hey, surfer dude? Surf is up!"

"Here I go-o-o," he shouted, as he squiggled and squirmed on the dock. Bam, he jumped up and raced back to grin and fidget beside me. What was his next ecstasy? Both of us kept laughing loud enough. His mother heard and stared.

"What are you doing? Leave that lady alone!" she yelled from another dock. She reeled in her fishing line and began a watch-out-for-mother walk towards the edge of her dock. I repressed my hilarity in the nick of time.

"No worries. We were having a blast playing games. He is pretending to be a surfer dude," I shouted back, from our nearby dock. Her son and I did not even try to stop the next giggles.

She watched, smiled, and returned to fishing while we played. Kudos for the Moms who go with the flow!

Something else happened. During our creative playtime, I remembered something else I read and never tired of rereading. Laugh hard, laugh soft. Today was exactly that kind of play day.

Hmmm, what about the cha-chings on my laugh meter? Soaring upward for sure! My heart felt splendid, ready to burst. No need to call 9-1-1.

What an outrageous number of laughs. Was it a no-brainer to embrace and celebrate my spring fever, an outdoor mania, and the hilarity of that splendid day?

Absolutely! No ifs, ands, or buts. My exceptional mantra for daily laughter worked incredibly.

But Wait, There is More...

Do not forego the unforgettable and appealing scenarios,
High time to interrupt the too-serious moments and pause for the rock 'n roll times,
Alas, a freer reign for a steady stream of cackles...

Have you seen the advertisements? Perhaps, way too many times? Morning, afternoon, or evening ads offer the latest, extravagant, and bizarre gadgets and the exotic products. Always guaranteed to make your life a total bliss—low maintenance and stress-free. Money-back guarantees to boot.

Do you mimic or make jokes during these ads? If I do not mute my remote, I am quite capable of a parroting behavior. Mimic an unforgettable line, bellow a miracle-product name, or give free reign to my humorous pantomimes and a steady stream of chuckles.

Remember the legendary hook for all the mind-blowing gadgets? ALL this miraculous stuff is only $19.95. But wait, there is more...

Wow, the perfect veggies for weeks. I had not forgotten my prized science projects. C'mon, they were yucky fun to discover. Now, my "fungus among us" would never grow again in any refrigerator with this special gadget. Never again?

Please listen, any television Googlers. Do not channel surf.

These magical containers and products are an incredible price. The entire loot comes with a freebie phone call and any flavor of credit card.

Who really cares? They do—the people who actually make a living doing these ads. Tune in. They pop up on additional channels during the commercial breaks. Alas, the hottest (no pun intended) product.

What about your unsightly, wrinkled clothes? You really want to spend this weekend doing piled-up ironing? But wait, there is more...

Another marvel is a pure delight. It is a one-hand only, given your effortless strokes. What comes next? Extraordinary attachments, ALL are only $19.95. Every gadget is *not available* in any store on our planet.

Excuse me. I did not mean to interrupt any comic relief that ensured an incredible laugh score. Easy, right? Easy to be headed for at least fifty-plus doses of lively chuckles.

Aha, a lot of squinting to read the 30-day guarantee or the money back return. Alas, write down the website—after everyone is asleep.

If we own a mammoth television? Hey, no urgency for our bionic eyes. Plus, here comes the next magical gadget and the mind-boggling extras. 'Tis the whole shebang and is only $19.95. But wait, there is more…

Do not let me disturb these rock 'n roll moments. Just like the professionals have noticed, there are the hours or days when we take ourselves far too seriously. I pay attention and change things, especially when I think seriousness is ruling the roost.

I intend to hold my stomach and gasp for the breaths, while emitting the stranger-than-fiction giggles. I adore this relaxation. My laugh-stats take an unforgettable surge upward to 145 times (daytime or evening).

Do any of us really buy this $19.95 stuff? Well, it is appeasing to know that other earthlings and myself are probably laughing in these supposed bonus moments on television.

None of us needs the contemporary insights. We attest that these minutes give our stomachs an aerobic workout, especially if we continue the rambunctious laughter.

Time for the mini-confessional. How many gadgets or miracle products did I order at a meager $19.95? One, maybe two…

Did you ever order the miracle products? Never-ever sharpen knives, super-fast dicers, a sham to beat all shams known to humankind, a gargantuan robe that covers drafty holes, or a different host of stuff. Buy pronto. Whichever "thang" on these ads is esplendido, better call now.

Remember? These marvels of our world or the universe (sic) are not in *any* stores.

Any of us still giggling and hooting? Who is in possession of the remote control? Pressing mute? Volume up? Aha, your significant other is calling again. Your children or teens are doing what?

Gales of laughter make it too noisy to hear the rest of the advertisement. Are we worrying or obsessing? Heck, no! Are we trying too hard to be right or perfect? Not today!

Let 'em rip—the feel-so-good gales of giggles. Now, our laugh statistics are growing unpredictably, exponentially, and more magically than any of these televised wonder-gadgets.

Hate to interrupt such appealing minutes, but it is time to recreate that memorable ruckus. In unison, pretty please…

ALL these gadgets are only $19.95. But wait, there is more…

No Worries With Za-Za-Zoom

Enjoy the delirious antics and the funny hijinks,
Let the enchanting experiences invade as a top priority,
Pure hysteria, marvelous bellyaches, and no worries…

I adored my memoir of the za-za-zoom antics and hijinks. My enchanting experience transpired during my sell-and-buy spree. Three homes, three years, and the same town.

Bonkers or delirious? No, it was a time frame of fantastic deals and lower interest rates. Little did I suspect that another za-za-zoom escapade was on my horizon.

The third home raised the bar for my zoom memorabilia. My former partner and I just finished unpacking our last boxes when our neighborhood teens sprinted over to check out "who" bought the last available homestead.

"Hi! You the new neighbors?" Seeing our smiles and thumbs-up, one teen headed straight for his hopeful bait.

"You would not believe certain dogs in this neighborhood!" He stood tall, letting his gangly arms rest upon the high handle bars of his dynamite bike.

My readers probably surmised what we needed to do immediately. His declaration was a dare. Go ahead, just ask. They appeared to be the neighborhood teens that chomped at the bit (almost literally) to tell-all.

To admit that each of these curious teens stopped by regularly was an understatement. Of course, there was the ultimate adoration, as we stopped our yard chores. We remained a devoted audience and chimed in with witty asides, given the embellished stories and their hysterical, innovative pantomimes.

Fast forward. Same teens, a different week…

That illustrious afternoon, I was working in my home office. Our dogs, Beau and Rocky, started the woof-woof routine. I headed outdoors.

Of course, there was a prime reason. Our dogs spotted you know who.

Our neighborhood teens were primed to the max. They were attempting to head down our embankment on a slalom ski intended for waterskiing. Indeed, shake or scratch your head while envisioning this unhinged, whacky scenario.

The sight was pure hysteria. Non-stop laughs and snorts left me with a marvelous bellyache. Hey, all for a good cause: the fabulous cha-chings for my laugh meter surpassed the 145 times per day.

Hmm, any bewilderment as to what happened to the teens and their former let-us-tell-you-a-dog story? Not today, as their surf-and-turf skiing took a top priority. These engaged and talented teens switched playtimes swimmingly.

C'mon guys, what were they thinking while hopping on a slalom waterski? Could it be possible that all of them were in La-La land?

Quite simple! Today's priority for this teen playtime altered dramatically with the *supposed* opportune weather.

Our evening weather gifted us with a light snow. Magnifico conditions ensued for a tantalizing ski-and-turf. Ultra worries or fussing? Never…

Our neighborhood teens were destined to have a blast, regardless of the ski-and-turf conditions. They barely noticed that Beau, Rocky, and I had arrived on the entertaining scene.

Was I ready to head back to my home office? Nix that deal. I was beholden for my gusto with these afternoon funnies.

That afternoon was a spontaneous reprieve, a crescendo of surprises. I committed to get in the act with the teens and this outrageous entertainment.

These teens loved everything. My non-stop hoots, splendid howls, and thumbs-up signs enticed the Olympian-caliber, winter acrobatics and their comical improv show.

Skirting their own pack of dogs and the addition of my eager-to-play Beau and Rocky on the ski-and-turf conditions became a crackerjack feat. Did their zany maneuvers eventually run amuck?

Well, the ski-and-turf challenges were getting to be a bit much. But never fear, the teen playtime was in max overdrive.

All of us za-za-zoomed from the ski-and-turf playtime back to the outstanding dog sagas. Aha, recall that it took only one teen to hook us with our neighborhood stories? Indeed, one teen dazzled all his buddies and myself with his slapstick recreations.

"Hey, listen up to the best-ever dog saga. You're gonna luv-v-v this one."

He za-za-zoomed right to his mimicry of "the growler." She rarely snapped or fought with neighborhood dogs, but still managed to have a say. No big deal, until her dog-lips got stuck on her gums. She would desperately try to get them back to doggie-normal.

I adored this goofus, dog-lip phenomenon. Personal laugh tallies were guaranteed to increase astronomically, as I recaptured and demonstrated these doggie images for several weeks.

It was refreshing that it only took one teen's exotic impressions to leave all of us in stitches. This uninhibited teenager had risen to the Oscar-time moments. He was on a roll, having no sympathy for our teary eyes, any stomach-holding, and our supremo tummy-aches.

Was he was right? Indeed, we were "gonna luv-v-v" his storytelling and imaginative mimicry in the company of our stellar bellyaches.

I basked immediately with my heartfelt memorabilia, chuckling softly as I wrote today. I still cherished his tell-all story and superb, down pat mimicry.

On any given hour or day, these teens were the masters of a pizzazz in life. They were committed to za-za-zoom and something else that was funny, boarding on riotous.

Life's pizzazz and their amusements were a persuasive code for living in that special hour, the outstanding minutes, or even the precious seconds.

Since those memorable times, I have moved to different states. I brought along this living-large code from those ingenious, delightful teens. No matter what day, month, or year, we adults make a choice to maximize our za-za-zoom scenarios.

Remember those measly four laughs per day for most adults? Well, a fond adios to that low average. In our fast-paced, frenzied, and undulating world, why not a medley of za-za-zoom pursuits to attain our mega-doses of daily humor?

No need to keep a hush-hush mindset. Several adults yearn to attain or surpass these youthful statistics of 145 times per day. When we want to raise havoc and increase our "adult stats" to an outrageous number of times per day, we are often ready. We anticipate, observe, and bust loose.

There are certain times for these idolized spaces and our playtime. We catapult with an evolution of the merriment, pranks, shenanigans, and our joviality. Even children or teens cannot stop us, only in their wildest dreams.

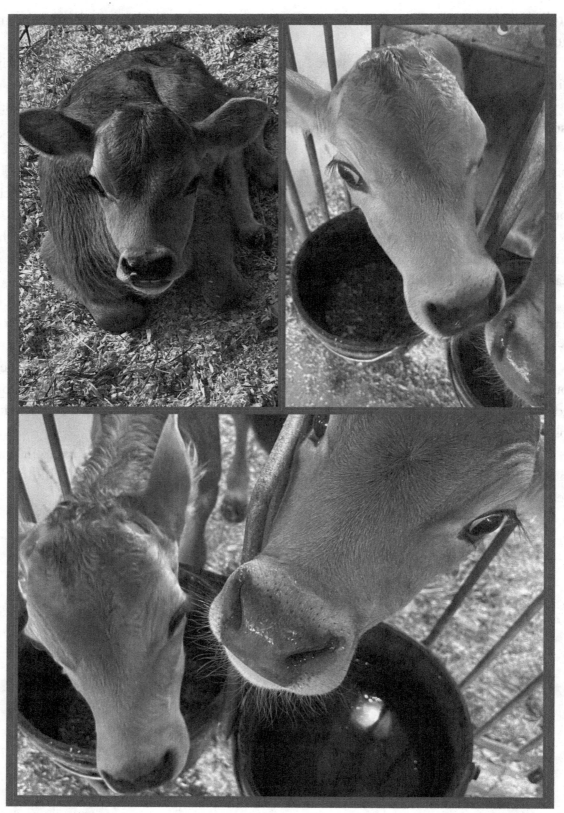

Engage with a peek-a-boo realm of no inhibitions and maximize our za-za-zoom playtime…

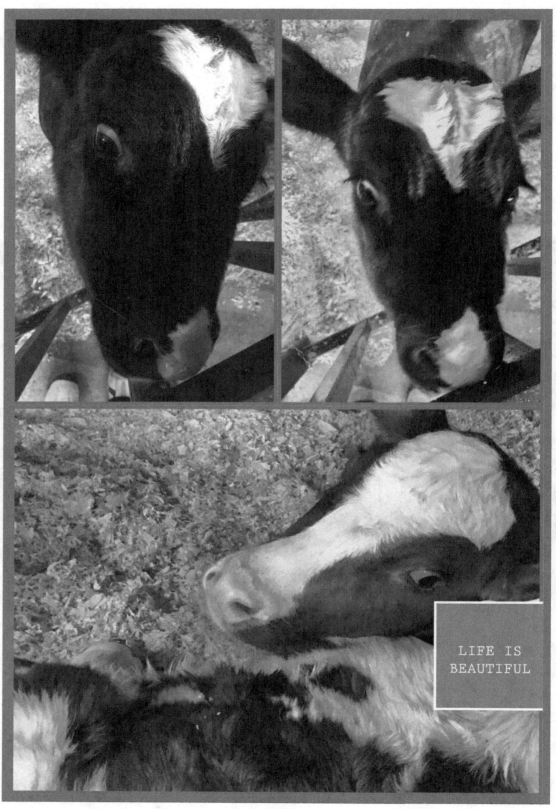

LIFE IS
BEAUTIFUL

Life is beautiful. We catapult with an unexpected and comical
photo, the diverse shenanigans, and our joviality.

Psyched Out-t-t

Let the bona fide reasons to remain psyched morph into our stellar fixations,
Let a mission of togetherness defuse the get-outta-of-here daily or weekly stressors,
Cherish that these vibrant minutes of our comical hours hours make a quality difference…

Can any of us unearth or recall those Groucho Marx glasses with the outlandish, kooky nose? I lost mine.

No need to fret, fuss, or get into a dither. My replacement glasses caused a few heckles, immediate hoots, and the razzing.

My rubbery-blue frames sported the miniature holes to see through the *psychedelic* glasses. They became definite keepers, not to be lost or tossed out for the rest of my life span.

I wore these funky, bizarre glasses to my faculty-student classes, acting like everything was normal. I dared to sport 'em the entire class. I did not take myself too seriously, as laughter was in my family DNA.

Across the months of any semester, my non-traditional and the traditional-age students touted that I was not a crazed, but an unexpected, fun-loving professor. They caught my contagious and go-viral spirit.

Early in the semester, my students knew that I was eager to incorporate role plays and simulation-gaming teachings. I favored the techniques for better assimilation and retention, enhanced motivation, potential humor, and our mutual inspiration.

Innovative teaching was my destiny. My wheel of fortune and teacher role models were cherished. Credible research supported at least seven learning styles. I scampered to include, celebrate, relish, and even luxuriate with these transformational and diverse learning styles.

Way back yonder, my college classes were a "new normal" for my students. Their different ages and varied cultures created something else. They pegged me as "wicked different" throughout their years of academic wayfaring.

By the end of each semester, the bravado notes with a signature and humorous anecdotes were taped on my office door. Other weeks, the notes were discovered on my desk.

Brownie points? Nope!

Across the decades, my oral and written evaluations affirmed that I was a tough cookie, but a fair professor. They noted that I was different, but qualified me as "a special prof" in their life globe-trotting and academic circles.

Their critiques were minimal, but enhanced my teaching modalities—for the next wave of intriguing students. At least these new allies snagged a "grapevine" for their exotic stories, but never the guarantees of a repetition.

My best-ever lessons? Laugh together, either softly or loudly. Never dismiss a multitude of opportunities to up the ante for our healthy 145-plus giggles per day.

There was a bona fide reason to remain psyched. Our mission of togetherness in classes and frequent visits defused the get-outta-of-here stressors. The vibrant minutes or our comical hours made a quality difference.

Promises to my students morphed into the positive affirmations. We traversed the mountain tops for the exemplary learning. We favored a commitment to a "tango on" in our classes. We did not judge the whoops moments, the sundry commentaries, and lively experiences along our rites of passage.

Throughout my impassioned career, there were validations of my personal beliefs. Open-minded professors remained humble and diehard students, endorsing the reciprocal learnings in their diversified classes. We seized an ownership of a forceful, intrinsic potential to laugh together.

Psyched out-t-t? That steamroller feeling became an understatement across my decades of teaching. The rewarding insights, meaningful connections, and intoxicating, enriching laughter transposed into our unforeseen treasures.

Let a luminous moon beget the hope and a celestial light over any darkness or despair…

Bucket List Extravaganza

Be adventuresome, valiant, and an enterprising soul,
Let the "aha" moments burst onto the scene,
Travel somewhere or some place never experienced or never googled…

There was a wondrous beacon of light. I cannot remember where I heard or read the appealing idea. This encouragement occurred during an enchanting springtime and grabbed my attention in a New York minute.

Travel *somewhere* that we *never* had been, especially once a year. Be adventuresome, valiant, or enterprising. These energetic qualifiers were enough, an endorsement for my self-care and self-love values.

Did our global pandemic alter this kind of encouragement? Would enough of us expand our bucket list extravaganza?

Well, millions of people were flying and driving to tempting locales, festive celebrations, fun-packed vacations, and their long-awaited, family gatherings. Enticing stories and sensational images were trendy, a distinct surge in the late spring and the summer of 2021 and 2022.

Breaking news featured these local to international treks and our appreciative rejuvenations. These ever-expanding events were captive headliners along with our next waves of exotic mutations.

Our low and high tides were changing again. Yet, the "millions of us" were seeking or planning these journeys.

By early September, the enchanting Cathedral of the Pines in New Hampshire was my lure. My semi-plans? A yummy picnic lunch…wherever.

An eve pitstop at a hometown diner? Or a venture to that magical eatery that we savored with my Nana and Gramps?

Whenever there was my dismissal of any schedules, I often snagged a unique playtime. Of course, I surrendered to today's bucket list extravaganza and the humorous experiences.

My PJ diva adventures were envisioned. I yearned to pursue the fun, meandering pathways and the newest trails near my parents' resting haven. A never-seen museum and mini-gift bungalow at the Cathedral of the Pines were another possibility.

No order or frantic pace to do everything. I declared no time constraints, just adventures galore. Good thing!

Forget googling the directions. My handwritten notes that worked the last ten years were snatched as I departed from my home. Forget that my GPS needed another update. My visual recollections would be spot on.

Pardon me, did I think that my semi-plans were superior? Ha! Superb ha-ha's would be forthcoming. I was laughing at and with myself that entire day and the evening.

Yikes! I was traveling way too far on one interstate. Thankfully, an "aha" moment burst on my scene. A month ago, my dear buddy reminded me that our wassup-Massachusetts trendsetters changed ALL of our exit numbers.

Changes for the better? Exit seven was fifty-something headed his way. It was even worse on the number differences heading north on this sunny, magnificent day. Indeed, I was going to be traveling *somewhere* that I had *never* seen.

My half-giggles erupted, as I veered off the interstate. Yay, no horn-beeping scenarios, just smooth sailing into this brand new surrounding.

"Hey, how timely! My speedy exit turned out to be a rest area," I touted, between a few cackles and patting my dash board. While waiting to park my beloved Galactica Goddess, my reflections returned to family. Like our family tradition, I adored the brainstorming of the creative or way-out namesakes for our trucks and cars.

"Herman" was our treasured, family convertible on a deluge of *somewhere* adventures. As I waited a bit longer to park beloved Galactica Goddess, here came my humorous flashbacks.

My Mom and Dad brought us on these lost-and-found adventures, without a GPS and my Dad's forget-the-maps (sic) missions. Rest areas with a few picnic tables or Dad's itchy Navy blanket ruled supremo. A wicker picnic basket, funky plates and utensils, and homemade punch in an old-fashioned jug with rattling ice cubes topped our adventuresome spirit.

Our mad dashes to the woods for a potty break remained a vivid recollection. On one escapade, a gargantuan dog investigated. He planted a frigid nose on my wee tush! I shouted for my parents and two sisters, especially when he tried to lick my face.

Only Mom bolted my way with an attempted rescue and a "SHOO, shoo…GO away!" This bigger-than-life dog romped around playfully, coming back with its frigid nose planted on my wee tush. OMG!

Gales of laughter happened, much later with my storytelling. Today? Quite the hysteria with my memory-lane replays. Now…Fast forward to today's *somewhere* journey.

Wassup here? I finally got a place to park Galactica Goddess at this bustling rest stop. Hey, a real building with restrooms, but the colossal signs were posted.

CLOSED due to COVID. Please use OUTDOOR PORTABLE POTTY. Masks recommended, if not fully vaccinated.

"Well, our 'new normal' was still lurking. No worries, no problem. Ha, I mastered the wooded rest areas for eons," I proclaimed aloud, content with today's tee-heeing and my family memoir.

My pitstop was accomplished with a stupendous balance and my ha-ha echoes from my portable potty. I exited giggling, only to witness a nearby couple eyeballing me suspiciously.

I reflected for a few seconds. *No appreciation of my humor or maybe no exotic family recollections? Hey, I dunno! I am ready to trot back joyfully to my beloved Galactica Goddess.*

Back in divine Galactica Goddess, an intuitive moment enticed me to try my GPS. I knew to head south, until whatever exit.

"Hey, Ms. She-voice? You are in charge," I asserted, as I typed my destination and cackled way too much, trying to type speedily on my techno-device.

I was really snickering now. My *somewhere-you-have-never-been* became the baffling or unknown routes, the itty-bitty towns, and the serpentine roads. There was an awesome state forest that lead me astray, but closer to my New Hampshire haven with the breathtaking New Hampshire and Vermont mountain-vistas.

"*Never* seen this town, the historic homes and vintage barns, and the organic farms. Hey, the mosey-along speed limits were permitting me to partake," I murmured, feeling peaceful and a bit smug.

Well, no puzzle as to why I began a wishful and playful desire. "If only…I levitated and flew like a crow to those mountains." Meanwhile, I was musing again.

An endearing soul taught me that 143 meant I LOVE YOU. Every time I looked at my GPS arrival time, it was 1:43 p.m. Unbelievable and incredible in the same moment!

"A sign? I *love* you Madre and JJ, my fun-spirited parents. Please continue to be my guardian angels and let me arrive before the 5 p.m. closing. I yearn for my exploration of the new trails, visiting your symbolic plaques, and gazing at the Monadnock and Green mountains nearby the Bell tower. Perhaps, re-visiting the comforting chapel, too!" I summoned, driving with my endless smiles and a peaceful sensation in my heart.

The interruptions were entertaining. My glee and amusement happened, as I did u-turns or drove down a road, only to do the turnabouts with my GPS delays.

"Yo, Ms. GPS, I need the techno updates, babe!" Then my next "aha" moment appeared.

"Hey, I recognize a few names. Blink-of-the-eye and these sprawling towns of New England seem familiar. Wow, New Hampshire or perhaps not?" I remarked out loud, as if someone was going to answer.

One sure bet? I surpassed the lost-and-found laughter and raised my bar higher than 145 doses per day.

"Not there? Yet…" I repeated aloud. I viewed my arrival time displayed on my GPS.

I witnessed 1:43 p.m., feeling a stunning, inner solace. "I remember, Mom. Love, sweet love. That was your valued inspiration for the family and our world until ninety-seven years young," I murmured softly. "I believe that the heavenly bliss is full of love…sweet love!"

I pursued today's adventuring, my peals of laughter and joyous moments, and the intriguing sights along my new roadways. When I finally arrived, I needed a restroom ASAP. Oh my, the outside restroom at the chapel was locked.

Suddenly, I giggled and murmured aloud. "Hey woman, the woods are right here, chock full of majestic pine trees, striking birch trees, and the plentiful shrubs. Just turn and head into the forest."

Well, forget about my urgency to tinkle, especially as I turned around. A new mini-garden for children was near this outdoor restroom.

Suddenly, there were one, two, three, four, and five Monarch butterflies enveloping me. A charismatic-like, Monarch butterfly kept flying towards my face and lips. This unexpected phenomenon was radiant, glorious, and dazzling for at least fifteen minutes.

"I am recalling my animal totem created by an endearing student. My inner transformative spirit was no surprise—a butterfly!" I declared in a melodic voice, sensing that my former doctoral student Jean heard me from afar.

Somehow, I did not need the restroom in these enamored minutes. I snapped the random photos and tried a few videos. To seize this splendor of nature, my welcoming butterflies, and staying in the awesome moments were today's gifts. When I turned to head towards the main door of the chapel, I spotted a new mini-addition.

A knowing grin was plastered on my face. This addition was completed during our COVID pandemic. Outside the chapel entry was an artistic mini-house with glass doors, a roof, and a beckoning sign. "Give a book. Take a book."

I jogged back to Galactica Goddess, snagged a tote, and left my *Epiphanies* book. I took a fiction book from the top shelf. I did not give a flip about the morphing winds, now becoming rather gusty on the hilltop.

I cracked up. My long locks of hair went every which way, loosey-goosey on this hilltop. Finally, my hefty tug at the chapel door opened to another beauty, the renovated and historic chapel.

Wow! Updated with a lighter paint, yet still honoring the exquisite stone and wood fireplace. A new area for the bronze plaques, the office, and a basement museum were created from an unused area of the original chapel.

The staff was welcoming, as we swapped our stories of the history and beauty of this nonprofit property. The sun became a hypnotic prism on the glass case with the bronze namesakes.

I had purchased a plaque for my oldest sister who passed away unexpectedly at sixty-two from pancreatic cancer. Uncle Joe's bronze plaque was near her, as my Mom and Dad wanted to honor him for his volunteer service during World War II. He became a fighter pilot on several missions, only to be shot down with his burial at sea.

"Got it done during the difficult stages of our pandemic, Mom and Dad. Finally, I am here to gaze at my gifted bronze plaques of honor and love," I whispered, sensing that return of my inner peace and stillness.

"I believe that all of you are watching over me…" I began to murmur, my gentle voice trailing off. I was headed towards a restroom that I needed—in that exact moment.

In the indoor restroom, I started to grin and wonder. *Hmmm, how did I manage to forget? I dunno! Never mind. Get a move-on to the bungalow, before it was closed.*

I scurried to the charming bungalow used for a gift shop. Handwoven potholders were donated. Hooray, managed to snafu the last two potholders, the last green mug etched with pines, and a box of balsam fir scents. My PJ snafu-actions became the laughable moments for today's volunteer and a ripple effect for myself.

Onward! Stopped at the amazing Altar of the Nations with the Monadnock and Green Mountain vistas. The wind gusts dominated. Then the darker clouds changed to a beseeching, white puffery in a breath-taking and striking-blue sky.

Like an entranced and giggling kiddo, I scampered down the grass and stone pathways. I began to speak and chuckle along the paths.

"Mom and Dad—Madre and JJ—I am *finally* here! After *lotsa somewhere towns* and routes, I arrived ahead of the five p.m. bong!"

"Oh lovely, the dragon flies are following me. The North position of my animal totem. Thanks again, dearest Jean. OMG! Devoted wife and mother. The dragon fly just landed on your bronze plaque, Madre," I continued to profess, as I placed my right hand gently near our beloved friend. "It landed and kept resting on *mother!*"

On my pinky finger was THE ROCK, the family namesake for my mother's diamond ring. It was a surprise and the now-affordable gift from Dad on their 50th anniversary. Photos in these quintessential moments and my jive-dance spirit kept coming forth.

Nobody ever came way down to this beloved area, heading the other direction towards the additional pathways. Hmm, my prism light from THE ROCK and my dance spirit became a beguiling signal to head the other way. I mused momentarily about the passing visitors and their innermost thoughts.

Poor thang, she is a bit loco, like the rest of our world during these times of global crises. My dear, please continue to remain a dance spirit to your heart's content!

I was different, but not loco (sic). I proceeded with my jive-dancing, a medley of tunes coming into my heart. There were no gusty winds. Re-appearing burgundy and blue-winged dragon flies came to visit.

In a spontaneous moment, I glanced at my cell phone and knew to call a soul-filled person. There were plentiful laughs and shared joys, but never any dismissing of today's resplendent stories of my special sign. After talking, I paused to revive our memories.

We shared this cathedral beauty, blissful signs, and the intriguing acreage during many seasons. Undoubtedly, both of us would venture here again.

Winding trails, hiking, and back to the never-seen museum in the basement of the chapel were euphoric. The honoring of men and women in the military, the artists, and the writers were today's endowment. Decades ago, these men and women were keepers of the light—for all of us.

I got goose bumps the entire time. COVID-19 and our mutations versus this historic museum of hope and light, luminous over any darkness, angst, or despair. An amazing grace…

Our lifetime lessons breeze in and envelope us on any day. Namaste was penned in their museum book, as I placed my donation in a vintage box. Today's gift of inner peace came full circle to my heart, as I closed the door gently.

Now, a last pitstop (sic) and back outside before closing. I paused at the bell tower, honoring women in the diverse branches of their military service. There was an exquisite "Tree of Life" sculpture and flowing water at the base of the tower.

Through the arches of this stately, stone bell tower? The beautific mountains and a whispering breeze accompanied my gifted day of *somewhere* and the taking-my-breath-away moments. Serendipity…

Heading down the paths again, I had a meet-up with another volunteer for the grounds. He asked where I travelled and our stories emerged. I thanked him for the caring efforts of the staff and volunteers like himself. They gave back to this celebrated cathedral.

"Your mother and father's story is special. Your plaques for your older sister and uncle in our chapel are very thoughtful. Plus, you chose to be here, whenever your time comes," he expressed, revealing his twinkling eyes and a genial manner. He embellished the intriguing tidbits to his storytelling.

"Everyone has a story or two. Thanks for your stories as well. Indeed, I shall return in whatever season," I replied with a smile, as I turned to sprint down the beloved path to my parents' resting haven with bronze plaques. I always revisited…

I experienced a bucolic repose and knelt down to share personal keepsakes. I murmured my tales of today and the mega-doses of laughter.

"You raised each of us to be strong women. We are different. Yeah, good different! Been told "good different" during my lifespan—as a professor, with close friends and significant others, and even with strangers or acquaintances," I murmured. Namaste was my signature closure, always with a heartfelt smile and the tossed kisses to the sky.

Today, a purple-hue near the clouds was visible and the stronger gusts of winds started again. I began to giggle as I kept looking back, wondering if more intriguing signs would beckon.

Wind-blown across the hilltop and heading to Galactica Goddess, I chose to sit awhile and sip my lemon-water. The darkened clouds and the mighty gusts of winds continued. Fifteen minutes later?

A sun-kissed PJ and Galactica Goddess, my beloved Kia Soul, were aglow. Amazing grace returned. It was just like the glorious glow witnessed upon my arrival at The Cathedral of the Pines.

Time for a fond adieu. Perhaps, it was perfect timing to find a hometown diner? Nostalgic memories usurped my ebb and flow of a hometown diner.

Instead, I headed to a favorite eatery that our family cherished, especially with my Nana and Gramps. My young waitress, who laughed heartily when I offered her a pair of roller skates, made for a fun-filled dinner and my nostalgic reprieve.

Before departing, the covered-bridge entry and exit caught my utmost attention. Was it the exquisite decor of white lights and a full moon? Perhaps, it was my childhood memoir? No matter, as these appeals awakened and enticed my evening enchantment.

Like my childhood and adolescence, I called playfully to the ducks. They paddled quickly for my food from the goody basket left purposefully for the patrons that wanted to linger. Today's bucket list extravaganza was my idolized gift.

The transforming evening brought out my cosmic, celestial grins. A luminous moon hovered o'er Galactica Goddess and my happy-self. We cruised joyously along the winding roads during our homeward wayfaring.

Doggie Adoration

Let the "go green" efforts in varied towns be inspirational,
Take exploratory treks and outings to discover an unforeseen bounty of delights,
Commune, frolic, or cut loose with a potpourri of happy doggies and be adopted immediately…

My exploratory treks and outings on the new, walk-bicycle trails that meandered around a picturesque lake, the streams, and several towns became an unforeseen bounty. An abundance of trails were made from recycled tires, a peachy delight for my young-elder legs and frequent exercising.

Additional landscaping with unique trees and shrubs, lovely benches, and the posh trash-recycling reprieves were an obvious enhancement. All the "go green" efforts in varied towns were inspirational. These efforts brought forth my appreciative smiles, friendly waves, and my sojourns along these pleasant pathways.

Morning or early afternoon walkabouts held my nature surprises. I was overjoyed to meet a handful owners with exuberant doggies. All of us appreciated the local supporters and state monies dedicated to revive the historic acreage, especially during the COVID-19 pandemic. Without a doubt, the outdoors lured and soothed our souls.

As I came down the historic spur near a former bakery, there was a woman with a striking white dog. My attention wavered as a distressed cat or baby birds were heard. Looking up, I finally spotted the wooded vicinity, but not the exact tree.

The woman came over to ask if I had lost something. Suddenly, she heard the distressed noises and became concerned. Together, we became the potential rescuers.

Suddenly, Mama flew back from afar, across the spacious lake to bring the wanton food. We smiled at each other, two strangers who were on the same page.

Her dog already sensed that all was well again. She began to nuzzle my legs and relished my comforting strokes. Oh, these feel-good and frolickin' times brought back an instant memoir.

I owned humongous dogs with the charismatic and quirky personalities. No mystery as to why adults, adolescents, and children were enamored, as their playful nature and captivating all playmates were their forte (and an awe-inspiring gift, I believe).

This woman's dog must have known my former dogs. The lean-into-you style, especially with my lofty strokes, was a hoot. Her loving, squinted eyes foretold her doggie ecstasy.

"I can tell. You are a dog lover. Just look at how she adores your comforting pats!" the woman exuded, giving me a majestic grin.

"Sure does! Check out how she leans into me," I responded, with my spontaneous giggles.

Time flew. I was engaged completely in our moments. We chatted, played with her passionate dog, and shared names—just in case we met again on the wondrous, new walkways that all of us appreciated.

Her husband had died of COVID—19 about a year ago. She informed her sons that she was going to get a perfect companion, but already knew the dog would be female. She chuckled when she told me that part of her family story.

"I loved our sons and my husband. I really gave time to all of them. Now, it is my turn to have lots of attention and love," she declared, pausing briefly to check out my reaction.

She watched me toss back my head and chuckle effortlessly. We smiled and expressed how we appreciated this delightful meet-up and looked forward to another visit in the near future.

I glanced down to admire her dog staring at me. "I believe she is more than ready for our next visit," I asserted, as I leaned over to bestow a lingering, gentle pat.

Both of us waved goodbye, sporting our mutual grins. Why not? I was adored and definitely adopted.

Sound bites

~ ~Cultivate an astounding appetite for daily and evening
playtimes. Slip into a kinder consciousness~ ~

~ ~Invent a playful celebration with friends. Witness and encourage strangers
to join and add their colorful hues to the inventive moments~ ~

~ ~Be transparent. Dare to create your fan club for amusing
surprises and all of the eccentricities~ ~

~ ~Be spirited, free, and ready for playtime. Hand out invitations
to other charmed or enchanted individuals~ ~

~ ~Embrace that whenever each of us evolves with a light-hearted attitude, our enticing memoirs are being created. We pay forward an envied legacy~ ~

~ ~Join a spontaneous, whimsical party. Enjoy whoever comes to celebrate. Witness the elation, animation, and playful artistry~ ~

~ ~Spark the moments for a self-indulgent play. Prime your psyche for a looney-tunes extravaganza~ ~

An Ode to Stretching Our Smileage

Relive any quirky scenarios or jubilee celebrations,
Permit the fortuitous, unanticipated, or welcome chuckles to arrive in a jiffy,
Recycle a nirvana that still awakens the mind, body, and spirit…

It did not matter that it was an earlier book. I opened randomly to my book chapters.

Just peruse, relive my quirky writings, and smile regularly, feeling less urgency to be stressed. Certain days, our smiles morphed into a snicker or the fortuitous, unanticipated, or welcome chuckles.

Today, a rereading of the recycled, cinematic days of my life wayfaring happened. These flashbacks and lively anecdotes, like a techno-color and cinematic drama, kept me present in my playtime memoir.

My rushing, streamline flashbacks dropped anchor as I reread the anecdotes from a chapter entitled, "Whenever we had a day or evening to spare." That essence triggered today's memory lane of my nostalgic winters in a tropical Arcadia.

No wintry blasts in this fairyland. I indulged in a jiffy to explore the beguiling beaches and to seek the exotic palm trees. Across the months, I sported my funky spring or summer attire. Attending a potpourri of outdoor venues during the day or the evening, bewitching hours was charming.

Back at the ranch (sic), the snow storms blitzed my region and the neighboring states. Meanwhile, I bragged and snatched the opportunities, especially at this stage of my PJ safari. My choice was purposeful and a no brainer. Rent for three or four months in this fairyland-nirvana, while the nor'easter storms plummeted my home turf.

With this writing, I began to envision the mini-sagas on television. They were side-splitting entertainment, especially when there were no dangers or limited power outages back yonder. The wah-wah whoops scenes, the spiral-and-slither glides, and the almost a nose-dive splats were fun to imitate.

Purposeful mimicry came at my outdoor venues while dancing in my jazzy outfits befitting this tropical Shangri-La. Bystanders would be clapping with my dynamite antics. Several dance partners jested, "You must be a Yankee, but certainly a jiving, charming snowbird!"

Another nostalgic memoir was triggered by a rereading of my chapter with anecdotes about whenever we had a weekend to spare. I spent seductive and winsome months on my Italiano-stucco balcony, enticed by a sky art of the alluring, tropical sunsets. Then I went swimming and floating in the calming waters of the regal pool, witnessing the hypnotic moonbeams.

Inhaling ocean sea mists on my daily strolls along the pristine shorelines were re-envisioned. These lucid images kept me rereading, always with my effortless grins.

Another flashback were my plentiful days at those blissful beaches and collecting sea shells. I cherished my devout kiddo, affirmed readily by enthused youngsters. They became my cling-ons and played full tilt with our boisterous, amusing water games.

Today, a quintessential memory and my exceptional photos permitted the shrieks of merriment. This state preserve was experienced with a new friend. The "blow holes" in the cliffs and rock jetties caused the unexpected sprays at high tides. Forty foot sprays, our hollers, the saturation, and laughing hysterically were guaranteed—IF the right conditions prevailed. BINGO! My new friend and I nailed the magnifico timing.

That evening in my journal, I was grateful to be alive to my chockablock life, especially my four winter reprieves prior to our global pandemic. Maybe I shall not return to that paradisiacal Arcadia, given our plane travel-woes, my car transporter, the unanticipated closures (wherever or at home), and our ramped-up mutations.

I was not a Pollyanna. I still adored searching and stretching for the optimistic moments, days, or weeks. My positive intentions to return "somewhere warmer" during our nor'easter months remained at the tippy-top of my bucket list.

Positive vibes and not letting the negativism outweigh the opportune moments or my weeks were important, way ahead of our global pandemic. My survival of major health issues and pursuits of healing modalities, the thirteen-year caregiving of my beloved parents, and other rollercoaster scenarios inspired my "tango on" spirit.

Present. It was the real key to what any of us knew at this very second. Yesterday was already vamoose. Our future remained unknown.

Choices! Our ownership of today's milliseconds or not? Each of us was a free spirit, so personal choices cropped up.

"Sign me up" was no longer a cliche. My seconds of coupe de grace were worthwhile. Ditto for my hours, days, weeks, or my pursuits to relive any remarkable years. Personal intentions included my effervescent giggles, my best-ever tummy aches, and, of course, my smile wrinkles.

I made it to my tropical Arcadia again. My intentions became a spellbinding manifestation. An ode to stretching my smileage remained true-blue and unwavering.

**Permit smile wrinkles to deepen as our wishful intention morphs
into a Shangri-La of Mother Nature manifestations...**

Eureka

Be merry with an unexpected prank and the engaging, immune-boosting laughter,
Watch carefully for these compelling minutes of ecstasy,
Let no boundaries on age interfere with a precious eureka…

I was walking. As I rounded a bend in the trail, I saw a compelling, unanticipated face in a tree. I backed up quickly, snickering in these diverting and fun minutes. Then I snapped assorted photographs.

Spontaneous photos remained my rarity. I liked to peruse the uncommon medley, relaxing in the evening. I pressed onward, enjoying my walkabout. Unexpected minutes launched me to a mystical place for an arrival—of the next, intriguing eureka.

Another weekend, I travelled to a rocky shoreline. As I jumped to and fro like a loco-crazed kiddo, my impish friend took the whimsical snapshots. My long-legged shadow enticed a pleasurable amusement—that day, and, of course, whenever I wished to glimpse again at these light-hearted photos.

Another week in January was a brr walkabout, but my diehard inspiration to be outdoors ramped up. Oh yah, I bundled up. By the mid-afternoon, I texted my sister and best buddy an impromptu photo.

I did a double-take and conceded. My gangly legs were quite conspicuous. Alas, I wore men's jeans with a 36 in-seam for many moons (sic).

As I sent a glaring photo into cyberspace, it displayed the wicked long shadows of my elongated legs. Eureka! Laughing at and with myself felt esplendido.

Another weekend, I went visiting and frolicking. My stroll in this neighborhood brought forth the Pterodactyl screeches. Nearby neighbors owned these "Jurassic Park" birds.

Wintry blasts were gone, replaced with the enchanting sixty-degree sunbeams, today's gentle breezes, and my happy-camper strolls. That evening in his homestead, I spotted a wild shadow from a chandelier on his white ceiling.

Mesmerizing or spooky? Go figure—the exotic shadow looked like an alien. Just imagine a Pterodactyl image, an exclusive spoof for both of us.

I shall snap a photo of his chandelier-shadow Pterodactyl on a different evening.

Frolicking antics and chuckles with our reassuring, *human* embrace under that chandelier-shadow Pterodactyl still resonate.

Mesmerizing or spooky? Hmmm, our choice becomes a free-spirit reign.

Whenever we pause for fun instances to laugh and create our exotic stories, there is a freedom. We are joyful with the unexpected pranks and our engaging, immune-boosting laughter. Choosing to be young kiddos at heart and no boundaries on age are a welcome amnesty from any chaos or angst in our personal or global world.

Dare to take a stand for the quality time. Take a hiatus for the eureka moments. Imagine my Pterodactyl scenarios, but enliven an impassioned, fun-filled memoir.

Witness the euphoria that arises during a personalized eureka. Foster and nurture the blissful feelings that pop up. Savor the shock waves, a jolt, the suddenness, or the splendid eye-opener.

Mellow

Hooked by wild doggie diversions and a lofty madness,
Proud to own my chutzpah and acting plum loco,
Our PJ-doggie togetherness was mesmerizing and mellow, no worries or the earthly
boundaries…

My best buddy was joining me for an idolized reunion. It was a treasured time to celebrate our days, actually two weeks in the breathtaking mountains.

This lively tradition happened to be an earlier fall in New England. Radiant leaves appeared on the pastoral trees in our bucolic mountains. For two years, this festive reunion plus our winter get-togethers in the tropical climates were postponed.

The global pandemic continued to create a real and surreal attitude and altitude. The flourishing mutations affected personal choices regarding plane flights and travel destinations.

Finally, there were the re-openings, popular outdoor events, and more widespread vaccinations and boosters. My endearing buddy chose to take a direct flight, arrive in my beloved "Bean Town," and, of course, be picked up in my avant-garde style.

My Mars-orange car, nicknamed Galactica Goddess II, was indeed "a looker" and could be eyeballed immediately. My outfit was vibrant and offbeat. I hopped out my driver's door, waving wildly at my precious friend of fifty years.

The state cops were not in sight. Yeah! Our master plan was to meet at this departure level, not the usual mad hatter, arrival-zone. Voila`—for my PJ manifestation!

Everything else was a piece of cake and today's gifts—our comforting lodge, only minimal travelers in this off-season, and my epic intentions and manifestations. Retirees, forever buddies, and our intriguing adventurers were not taken for granted. An unexpected, early foliage of beauty ensured our adventuresome and unforgettable reunion. We were mellow, the upbeat playmates and the reunited, longtime friends.

We whizzed off to the ole' farms with the countrified, mountain vistas for the homegrown goodies and our tradition. The season's apple cider donuts in the company of our apple cider guzzles were splendiferous. Once again, our daily selfies and my photo collages were spot on.

Our playful reunion of two weeks was chock full of the consummate weather. Only one rainy day became a longer mellow day, but there was neither fretting nor fussing. Our medley of shared photos and videos from the past two years provided us with a wingding of entertainment.

Neither of us was known for the traditional photos. During the last year, his daughter wanted a puppy. That drizzling day, we were witnessing an array of doggie pics.

Hysteria and pleasurable tummy aches ensued with the photos of her melodramatic doggie. Before our high-spirited reunion flew by, I created the prized photo collages. As we displayed and cracked up with our darling photography albums, guess which photo collage topped our prime pick?

Cheerio and awesome, Mellow! I decreed that his namesake and theatrical poses needed to be our crowning, unsurpassable gift that rainy day.

Undoubtedly, my striking photo collage with Mellow's befitting attitude and doggie-altitude were a no-brainer. Our brouhaha laughter was inspirational and priceless. The joy evolved into an off-the-charts memoir of our grandiose reunion.

LIFE IS BEAUTIFUL

Optimism is a happiness magnet. If you stay positive, good things and good people will be drawn to you.

Share the brouhaha laughs, quintessential images, and a joyous reunion, enhancing the legacy of a priceless friendship...

On the QT

Been on the Internet lately? Searching for almost everything? Several of us welcomed that close friends, possibly a new friend or two, offered us the enterprising ideas or the impressive insights.

When they shared—on the QT—whatever they fancied, like a priceless YouTube video or an intriguing website, something else happened. This offering stirred a curiosity or perhaps, our insatiable passion.

Our personal mission and pursuits followed suit with the informative websites, hobbies to explore, new recipes, or whatever we fancied. Several of us searched earnestly for the comedic reliefs, especially when we coveted or craved a promising and cheery mood for that day or week.

A funny schtick, a farce, a lighter fare of entertainment, or the gratifying videos were appealing. Something stretched our imagination or tickled a funny bone. Our liberation and respites were advocated, especially with a global pandemic and our aftermath of an unpredictable wave of mutations.

Hope floated again. Diverse events and our gradual re-openings included the indoor and outdoor entertainment. My friend told me about a smaller event, on the QT, of course.

Shortly thereafter, I began my zealous mission. Explore the outdoor events that were not overcrowded, but venues that offered the sought-after jollies. And, of course, a stupefying joyfulness for my heart along with kindred playmates.

I pursued an outdoor venue with a western flair—the brutish bulls, genial cows, and the mini-shows for our lavish entertainment. From the smaller crowd, like a lightning flash, I was spotted by a handsome cowboy. He tipped his stately hat and meandered in my direction.

My heart emitted the racing mega-beats. The closer this dapper cowboy came, I just knew. Something else was brewing for me.

"Howdy, Ma'am," he drawled, revealing a charming smile and his awesome dimples. This suave cowboy held out a bronzed hand, clasping mine (oh, smashing). We strolled over to another lanky cowboy with his mighty powerhouse of a bull. Whoa, this stout bull was a Longhorn.

My bronzed cowboy grinned again at me, turning slowly towards a flourishing gathering of intrigued folks. They were nudging their friends or pointing to us, a captivating trio with that brutish bully wooly.

"Folks, I know this angelic woman rides stately horses. But, do you think this fine, dazzling equestrian wants to climb up on this *Longhorn* bull?" he challenged, as the intrigued crowd began clapping.

As if on a perfect cue, most of them bellowed, "YES!"

I played along, displaying a confident look, a dynamite pose, and my noticeable head nods. But, I was definitely keeping one eye on that untamed bull.

Hey, no direct eye contact. Living in Texas throughout my career, I was well versed with the do-not-stare forecasts regarding the wild, brutish bulls. No bull!

"I am FEARLESS!" I boomed in my finest voice, noting that the crowd was multiplying in number, hooting or howling, and clapping madly. I smiled like a Cheshire cat, but felt my lips sticking on my gums. I began to daydream.

Only in this daydream. Nervous? Never! Okay, just a tad. Yeah, my expressive Texan-talk emerged. I mused for a few milliseconds. Chill! Just the PJ nervous-excitement...

The lanky cowboy with the Longhorn bull was now offering his hand and the stirrup to mount up. Backtrack to my nervous-excitement and inner reflections.

Man, so-o-o glad that I have long-g-g legs. Bully wooly is huge, requiring a wicked swing of my right leg to reach his right side-stirrup. Hey, using one stirrup would be crazy! I need to master this feat ASAP, no cowboys to the rescue. Wassup? Am I hearing the louder gasps from the crowd?

"Yeehaw, folks! This woman is brave and talented," clamored my dimple-grinning cowboy. He was already laughing and jumping backwards.

This bully wooly? Tee-hee! He was relieving himself, shortly after I mounted spectacularly. The crowd went from their loud gasps to a wild applause and boisterous laughs.

I was relieved (no pun intended). This *Longhorn* bull was going nowhere. I continued to laugh deliriously.

Ditto happened with my handsome cowboys. My bully wooly, spectacular dismount had to be a show-stopper.

"I gotta miss his WHIZ=PUDDLE!" I blurted out, much to the delight of my amused, gratified cowboys. Yeah, I was enamored with my panache and my PJ gymnastic feat.

Wha La! My impressive dismounting and flawless landing, afar from the Longhorn's whiz-puddle, kept the clapping and lively crowd intoxicated. Or, so I daydreamed. After all, my cowboy friends were winking and smiling.

What a flamboyant, outdoor venue and a lustrous afternoon to be taken off-guard. I was awakened, in the best of ways.

There were rousing, exciting, impressive, and comical moments. Beyond a shadow of a doubt, there was a prime memory lane for all of us.

Angelic Surrender

The mystique of a telepathic message or symbolic signs make a grandiose entry,
This enlightening spirit caresses our mind, body, and soul ever so gently,
An honoring of guardians, archangels, and a poignant spirit engenders a noble and entrusted realm of surrender and our manifestation…

Each Monday, I read a newsletter from England. Today, there was an intrigue and mystique with a prelude about our angelic messages and the symbolic signs.

An affable, inquisitive, and enlightening spirit began to caress my mind, body, and soul ever so gently. I already entrusted and believed. My guardian angels and my loving messages or signs came forth, way ahead of these British communiques.

I honored the personal stories, never worrying or overthinking about my gift of heartfelt messages and symbolic signs. Later, I affirmed that my beliefs and experiences regarding the guardians, archangels, or ascended masters were accepted by other kindred humans. However, if there were doubts, worry, or disbeliefs for any readers, they were free to turn my book pages to a different or resonant story.

For sustained and pleasurable times in my life, I was aware and grateful with the unexpected or familiar signs, particularly from my parents and eldest sister. My heartfelt or unpredictable glimmers usually appeared as vibrant imagery. This vestige arrived prior to their eternal rest and, incredibly, several years after their deaths.

My poignant images and harbingers were intentions that manifested at different times in my lifespan. Gentle smiles came forth. My "thanks to each of you" and "namaste" were spoken softly or as an inner telepathy.

This particular afternoon? I began to snicker. My boot almost landed upon the shiny penny.

"Okay, JJ. I picked up your wicked shiny penny. You have been leaving me coins regularly, much like your beloved coin collection…" My murmuring continued, only interrupted by the feel-good snickers.

My Dad, nicknamed JJ by our family and his colleagues, was a prankster (an understatement). Right after his death, JJ bequeathed me the *fifteen* buckerooskis, plus another dollar for my companion. We found most of the monies, only as we walked behind his pickup and glanced at a leafy curbside.

Go figure! The crosswalk to our beloved coffee shop was in front of us. Neither of us conversed during those moments. Both of us just walked to that curbside and found a resplendent gift that unforgettable day.

My Dad, the prankster JJ, was into the "fifteen" signs for me for a longer time. That same day? My companion shared that he won sixteen dollars—only once in his lifespan.

Yeah, he found *one* buckerooski in the coffee shop on the wooden floor. Nobody in line lost one buck. We kept getting a multitude of images and signs, especially for a few months after JJ's death.

We were wide-eyed, gasping, or incredulous. "Do ya think…" Finally, we just surrendered to my Dad's signs. Our constant belly laughs with the unexpected messages or symbolic signs were accepted as comforting, loving surprises.

Eleven years later? I still was bequeathed with the coin signs. Telepathically, I made sure that JJ knew my readiness for a lotto winner. Okay, at least a scratch ticket that became a PJ winner (sic).

Across the years, my cloud images were primarily from my parents, sometimes my eldest sister. They were riveting and distinctive, whenever they flourished, on cue or not.

I paid homage to today's flashback with a reading from England and my angelic surrenders. I attended the online summits on archangels, guardian spirits, and ascended masters. The international, renowned leaders and diverse presenters from the metaphysical and neuroscience realms were valued.

My curiosity advanced and matured naturally. These unfeigned experiences elicited my grins and the subterranean noises from a deeper abyss of my blissful tummy.

Sound bites

~ ~Be smitten with a positivity that emanates from the ripples of the laugh vibrations. Electrify the mind, body, and spirit with a peppering energy~ ~

~ ~Follow the leader whose countenance is charismatic and amusing. Be gifted with this humor that often reveals a kinder and wiser soul~ ~

~ ~Let a lively IQ skyrocket with an intentional creativity. Brainstorm a new-fangled passion, ingenuity, or inspiration~ ~

~ ~Unearth and take stock of fun-filled minutes. Let the circadian rhythms readjust with this natural ebb and flow~ ~

~ ~Attend a laugh-aerobic workout. Experience the bounty of grin-win attitudes. Be infatuated by the quirky and comedic playmates~ ~

~ ~Cast out a somber mood. Reel in today's light-filled seconds, minutes, or hours~~

~ ~Adrenaline moments fill up with escapades and the lingering feel-great minutes. Liberate the mind, body, and spirit with the uplifting dramas~ ~

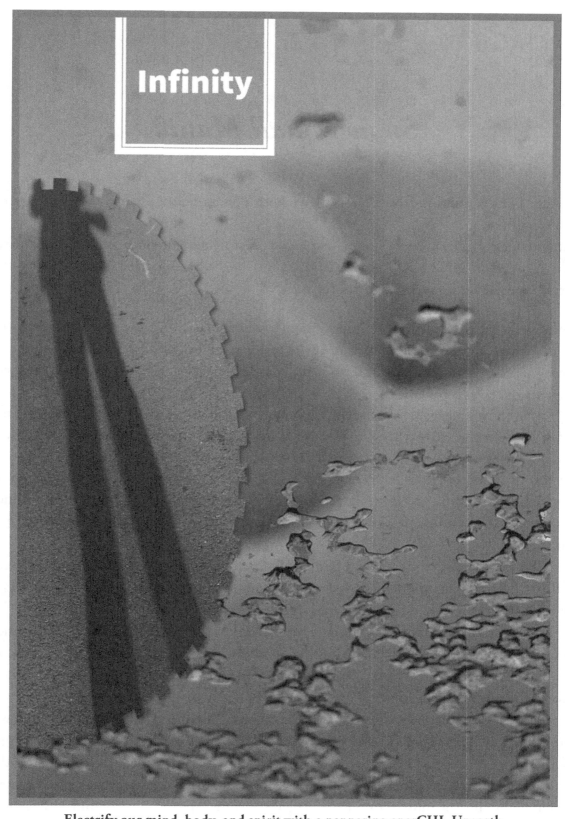

Infinity

Electrify our mind, body, and spirit with a peppering enerCHI. Unearth
and take stock of an infinite number of fun-filled minutes...

Snow Squall Mania

Mother Nature and her frosty blasts arrive with a tantamount energy, ever so brazenly and steadily,
Laughter and playtime come hither—when we least suspect the inconceivable fortunes,
Like-minded neighbors run 'round and 'round like whirling dervishes, ensuring the springtime memories of a delightful ruckus…

Unforeseen snow squalls, those imposing and wintry blasts, in the fine company of our monumental and lofty jubilation elate us. A phenomenal "out of the blue" cliche` awakens, taking us off-guard. Laughter and playtime come hither, especially when we least suspect these inconceivable fortunes.

I was living large, experiencing the whipping and walloping winds while tugging at my beret. I laughed heartily whenever I was chasing that airborne beret. Mother Earth Gaia and her frosty blasts arrived with a tantamount energy, brazenly and steadily.

Inconceivable fortunes happened during this snow squall. My like-minded neighbors donated to my rowdy, uncontrollable laughter. They decided to run 'round and 'round. We became the whirling dervishes in tandem or the loco earthlings who were undeniably out of sync.

Which spirited earthling would be able to clinch my fleeting, quasi-aeronautical beret in this snow squall mania? What a ruckus afternoon in concert with the leftover memories for each of us to revive, when our tamer spring appeared.

I gave our maintenance crew the deserving acclaims to fame and another crazed dance during that blustery plow day. During the next few days, I cooked and bequeathed my familial goodies of a savory pumpkin bread and a mouthwatering fudge for their valiant efforts and admirable attitudes.

I lauded our fortunes. The not-so-stellar stories abounded with the abodes down the street and their unpredictable plow crews. Sentiments expressed by those residents, acquaintances, and friends heightened a genuine appreciation and my evolving gratitude.

Our unique maintenance crew was laughing or joking, no matter what season greeted us. Undoubtedly, the mutual tidbits and engaging stories made a quality difference in our daily living experiences.

Other forecasted storms were blitzing us in the upcoming months. Snow squalls and a definite potential for the next bouts of our neighborhood mania morphed into our winter-wonderland melodramas.

OMG! Alas, my readers were now privy as to why I was already smiling, snickering, and envisioning the notorious bellyaches.

Earth Angel Canchetta

Surrender to the bliss of becoming,
Partake of the unexpected storytelling with a stranger,
EnJOY the exquisite milliseconds and lasting minutes of mutual gratification…

I was on the verge of deleting an unfamiliar phone number and the voicemail. Suddenly, my intuitive vibe kicked up a notch for a spectacular moment. My intuitive vibes were rarely overlooked.

There is no such thing as no coincidence. So, I made a perceptive choice and listened.

Hurrah! It was a meaningful message about my investment changes. I tried to call back and got the notorious recording.

"I am unavailable. Please leave your detailed questions and a phone number." I left a hopeful and detailed message, while performing a humorous pantomime, given the daily reality of our robotic techno-world.

A postscript was warranted. I amused myself on most days with a comical mimicry of any robotic voice.

An intuitive vibe arrived again, just before I opened a patio door to depart for the afternoon. I paused for mere seconds, sat down on my cushy couch, and dialed again. As the phone rang, I started to muse.

Third time is a charm. Try the number again. Oh well, my second call was dropped right away. Hmmm, I shall try a third time for my charm. Alas, a human voice is answering. Actually, it is a melodic and very kind voice.

Yah, it worked to pay attention to my intuition. I truly felt that I would reach a real human being with my third attempt.

A quick update with my name, my recent voicemail, and within a few minutes, Chanchetta and I were on a roll. Between the important verifications and DocuSign on my laptop, both of us engaged in personal asides that just happened. Of course, there is no such thing as no coincidence.

Our sisters passed away unexpectedly at younger ages. We were the definite empaths to each other. A few minutes were devoted to these enriching memories with our sisters while the PDF downloads for my investments happened.

"Our memories can never be taken away from us." Both of us relayed this identical expression of gratitude.

"We had a closeness in our families that some people never experience or ever know, even if our sisters were an unexpected loss and a real mourning."

My earth angel Chanchetta agreed. Both of valued our familial gratitude.

We shared more sound bites about the exceptional memories of the fun-loving times with our sisters. It was amazing. My Mom, Dad, and her grandmother affirmed the stellar lifelines to 96 and 97-plus years in the company of their memories.

"They will outlive us, most likely. Or, maybe not? Hey, none of us knows…" I quipped, permitting my chuckles to stream across our phone line. These light-hearted commentaries brought out today's giggles and our hearty, appreciative laughter.

Chanchetta was today's earth angel. I was quick to inform and compliment her, as we would probably not talk again. Her response?

"You put a smile in my heart! Thank *you*."

"Chanchetta, a smile is plastered on my face. There is a treasured ditto, that precious smile in my heart, too."

After we hung up, I lingered upon my cushy couch with a blithesome grin. Mellowing out felt natural. I knew and entrusted. I untied a beautiful ribbon and received my unforeseen gift for today.

Chanchetta and I became the empaths and laugh buddies. Just two strangers? Just a telephone conversation?

What a consummate and crowning day! Today, our compassion and mutual laughter transformed into a dynamic-duo scenario. Our luster was never forgotten.

My classic belief came full circle across the tides of time. Indeed, there was no such thing as no coincidence.

Permit a space for the new empaths and laugh buddies. Remember the unexpected snapshots. Never say never. There is no such thing as no coincidence...

Epilogue

Amusing faces and engaging scenarios become our gallery of colorful imagery,
Now suited to accept our imperfections with an authentic self-love and self-care,
An enrichment to the world with our blithesome, obvious rise and daring leaps of faith…

Recall the split-seconds or the unforgettable moments. Perhaps, there is an entire day with our feisty attitude and that marvelous merriment. Perhaps, there is a gifted week of our exceptional amusements.

Enjoy that unmistakable zest accompanying this realm of free spirit. Gonzo, rambunctious, rollicking, or raucous breeze into our life and drop anchor. We succumb to this wild-thang mindset and a timely arrival of our playful vibes.

Go ahead and grab a notepad, iPad, laptop, or whatever. Just compose or scribble the light-hearted stories or a few sound bites to capture those exact moments.

Create an ole' fashioned diary. Perhaps, there is an innate desire to journal daily or weekly. These ruckus stories or the spontaneous moments without a price tag—our wild giggles or outrageous hilarity—are sustainable. Incredibly, these moments summon and coax our inner, attentive spirit.

Fuel our soul. Let our Tao of healing become laughter. Become soul-filled to the brim. Let our goblet runneth over.

Pause again to feel that free-spirited and elated nature. Nurture, nudge, or invite a feisty soulmate, close friends, or the new-found acquaintances.

Partake of these lofty and chipper moments of "now." Any of our companionate folks already own the witty, diverting mindsets. They promise an instant guarantee.

These individuals entice and heighten a jovial storytelling and our natural composting. These like-minded people morph into our earth angels.

They befriend, bolster, and encourage. They help us to sustain our writing-fever or a jolly storytelling with a comic relief, the flamboyant laughter, and our delirious euphoria.

Befriend the earth angels that inspire and encourage us to pause and reflect upon our choice of a free spirit. They entice and sustain our jovial stories, writing, and journaling…

My first story or journaling about the lofty, bombastic, and the flamboyant laughter…

My second story or journaling about the hilarious, bodacious, and the fun-lovin' memories...

My third story or journaling about the tummy-ache moments of ecstasy and the delirious euphoria...

Discover your keepsakes like a rough-cut gem that bequeaths the chakra
hues and the sun-kissed shells gifted by Mother Earth Gaia…